After Adoption

Working with adoptive families

Edited by Rena Phillips and
Emma McWilliam

B	*ritish*
A	*gencies*
for A	*doption*
and F	*ostering*

Published by
British Agencies for Adoption & Fostering
(BAAF)
Skyline House
200 Union Street
London SE1 0LX

© BAAF 1996

Charity registration 275689

**British Library Cataloguing in Publication
Data**
A catalogue record for this book is available
from the British Library

ISBN 1 873868 27 8

Designed by Andrew Haig & Associates
Cover illustration by Andrew Haig
Typeset by Avon Dataset Ltd, Bidford on Avon
Printed by Russell Press Ltd. (TU),
Nottingham

Contents

Foreword

Phillida Sawbridge

Every paper in this collection bears witness to the fact that the placement of a child in a family, and the legalising of an adoption, are only the beginning of the story, and that in real life not even social workers can sign off with a cheery 'and they all lived happily ever after.'

Many adoptive families do, of course, live as happily as any other family, whatever that means; but present-day adoptions tend to be as challenging a way of creating a family as one could devise. So many of the children now being adopted have had experience of neglect or abuse, and join their new families desperately needing healing and normality; but as likely as not they are so hurt and fearful, suspicious and resistant that their new parents face an uphill struggle.

There can and should be no signing-off by people who have been instrumental in arranging such adoptions, or who have been important to the participants, particularly the child, in the past. No longer can it be argued (if indeed it ever should have been) that adoptive families are just like every other family and should be left to make their way through life like everybody else.

When parents take on children whose life-experiences have been so destructive that they have had to be removed from their original families, they are not entering into normal family life. Those responsible for deciding that the future of such a child lies within a family surely have the long-term responsibility of helping to make it work. They cannot pull out saying there are no resources for further involvement, which is, all too often, seen as the deciding factor. That is like saying that we have bought a car but have no money to fill it up with petrol or oil, or to license or service it. If we buy a car, we have presumably arranged our budget to allow us to run it. So it should be with planning for children. Post-adoption services are not an additional extra, or a luxury. They are an essential part of the provision, ensuring that the placement has as good a chance of succeeding as it can possibly have.

We have only to look at the alternatives to see the sense of this. Firstly, the breakdown rate in adoptions of older children and those with special needs is known to be high, and support services to be minimal. The cost to a child of suffering what inevitably feels like a further failure and rejection if a placement breaks down probably cannot be estimated. The financial cost is enormous too. Residential or foster care doubtless follow, at least for a period of time, along with costly case conferences and a concentrated input of resources while the breakdown is being sorted out. If the child remains in care for any length of time, the cost almost certainly far exceeds what would have been spent on that child's share of an effective post-adoption support service to the whole family.

This collection of papers sets out a wide range of thinking about the need for post-adoption services to adoptive families; about what they would like and how it should be delivered; about how adopted young people feel, especially when transracially adopted; about the need for good assessment, preparation and training, and about how services need to adapt to changes in adoption such as continuing contact (or "openness"). There are models, descriptions of good practice, accounts of how participants feel, and analyses of different helping approaches. An agency or department wanting to construct a really good post-adoption service would not go far wrong to base it on a careful study of these papers. Caroline Archer, in her paper, says, 'What parents living with such troubled children do need *is to be listened to, to be believed and to be empowered . . .*' At the very least, we can all try to hear what these authors are saying to us, believe they know what they are talking about, and use what we hear to help us empower those people who are taking on one of the most challenging tasks in modern life to do the job successfully.

Introduction

Rena Phillips and Emma McWilliam

Rena Phillips is Lecturer in Social Work, at the Department of Applied Social Science, Stirling University. Emma McWilliam is Professional Officer, Adoption and Fostering, Central Region Social Work Services.

In 1988, BAAF published a book on post-adoption services optimistically titled *Keeping the Doors Open*. At that time, the view that adoption goes on for ever and that adoptive families have a right to a service which does not end when an adoption order is made, was just coming into focus. Some voluntary and statutory agencies were beginning to respond to the need for post-adoption services, but alarm bells were beginning to ring about the problems of resourcing this area of work.

In the mid 1990s, post-adoption services are at a critical point. On the one hand recognition of their importance is gathering momentum, and on the other they continue to suffer from a lack of funding. Further, there is widespread disappointment and frustration amongst adoption agencies at the absence of any proposal in the White Papers on the Adoption Law Review to develop post-adoption services, with good practice expected on a nil cost basis. The result is a patchy development of services. For a large number of families there is little ongoing support offered. Yet in some areas imaginative specialist services, particularly in the voluntary sector, have been established. To keep up the pressure for a comprehensive post-adoption service we need to share and exchange with each other both our achievements and shortcomings. Most importantly, practitioners are continuing to learn about the challenges and problems facing adoptive families, and the kind of post-adoption services they require – in the words of one contributor in this collection, 'parents are indeed the experts on their own child'.

This book is the first publication in Britain to concentrate solely on post-adoption support for adoptive families (as opposed to other members of the adoption triangle). Their needs are significantly distinct and

1

special to merit a separate examination in greater depth. A wide range of issues and perspectives are covered. At the same time a number of common themes run through the chapters. These are:

- A focus on the views and experiences of adoptive families;
- The "hit and miss" nature of post-adoption services;
- The range of services required not only from social work agencies, but education and health services, both in the statutory and voluntary sectors;
- The need for cultural sensitivity in providing services in view of the specific requirements of families from black and minority ethnic groups;
- The development of progressive practice and innovative models of support.

Themes covered

When an adoption placement disrupts the reasons can frequently be traced to the lack of a comprehensive assessment of the child. This in turn can lead to a lack of "fit" with the adoptive family. Effective pre-placement assessment and preparation of families and children is a vital foundation for post-adoption support. The opening chapter offers a model of assessment and matching, developed by a voluntary agency, which aims to prepare the child and family for placement. In the following chapter, the sensitive question of financial support for families is raised by examining a flexible and responsive use of adoption allowances.

The next two sections are concerned exclusively with users' views. Get any group of adopters together and the subject of schools is bound to crop up, reflecting their strong concerns about meeting the educational needs of their adopted children. In Section II we hear from families about why they so often find themselves in conflict with schools regarding their children's education, issues around special needs education, and the experience of using residential schooling. Section III presents the reality and pain of day-to-day living with children suffering from the long-term effects of separation, abuse and attachment disorders and the kinds of support which help families to sustain difficult adoption placements.

Adoption never takes place at a fixed moment in time. Problems and needs change, and some phases are more difficult than others. For the adopted adolescent attachment, separation, identity formation, independence/dependence conflicts and sexuality are some key issues. Section IV looks at how adolescents and their families can be helped to survive what can be a most testing time.

Families who adopt children with emotional or behavioural difficulties need regular breaks just as much as families who adopt children who are physically disabled or have learning difficulties. The challenge is to provide short-term care which offers a positive experience for the child as well as a break for the adoptive family. However, family based schemes geared to adopted children are thin on the ground; one such scheme is described in Section V. We hoped to find examples of respite care such as home support services and adventure based holidays but it proved difficult to locate families who have benefited from such services, indicating a real gap in flexible and imaginative short-term breaks.

Troubled children also need therapeutic help, but again the picture is of services in very short supply. Additionally, there are many obstacles for families to overcome in seeking the appropriate therapeutic intervention – will the right kind of help be available? Where do you go to? Who will pay for it? Can therapy make a significant difference? A rich variety of therapeutic techniques and perspectives are described in Section VI. As one contributor rightly points out, there is no single approach to the management of behavioural and emotional problems of adopted children; different approaches suit different children at different times. Therapists may disagree with each other, but the common link between the contributors who discuss therapeutic help, is their interest in adoption and their enthusiasm and commitment in working with adoptive families and adoption agencies.

It is anticipated that recent developments in adoption practice will place additional demands on post-adoption services. The move towards open adoption, particularly in cases of face-to-face contact, presents adoption agencies with new challenges on how to prepare birth parents and adopters for a potentially difficult situation. Section VII examines how arrangements for openness are being managed, and what resource implications exist for the continued involvement of practitioners in newly established open adoptions and in "opening up" closed adoptions. Families speak about living with openness, including an open situation in a transracial placement, and the support they need for this new dimension in adoption.

As social work is becoming increasingly sensitive to the ways in which its practice can play a crucial role in combating discrimination, further challenges will be posed by the placement needs of black children and those from other minority ethnic groups. In Section VIII, a mixed race couple who have adopted a mixed race child describe the hostility and racism they met as part of their post-adoption experience. In the context of the transracial versus same race placement debate, and the requirement of the Children Act 1989 and the Children (Scotland) Act 1995 to give due consideration to a child's racial origin and cultural background, a black post-adoption worker explores, with the help of poetry, the long-term issues of a child's ethnic and racial identity. She describes the setting up of a group for transracially adopted young people, and a black adopted person explores personal issues of identity. Most intercountry adoptions are also transracial. Post-adoption issues in intercountry adoption may include difficulties with identity, as well as the need for background information in order to be able to answer children's future questions about their origins – these are explored in Section IX. There is a need to ensure that intercountry adopters are not excluded from post-adoption developments.

In order to prepare adopters, and importantly, practitioners as well, for a developing and complex post-adoption scene, ongoing training is essential. In the concluding chapter, recent post-adoption training programmes set up for adoptive parents and social workers by BAAF's Scottish Centre are evaluated. The clear message is that adopters appreciate training which is of a practical nature and which addresses directly the problems they are struggling with day to day.

1 A model of assessment and matching

Carol Douglas

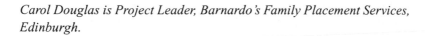

Carol Douglas is Project Leader, Barnardo's Family Placement Services, Edinburgh.

Adoption of older children and children with "special needs" is an inherently risky business. It is our responsibility as workers in adoption agencies to take risks on behalf of children in need of family placement. A fine judgement of risks is called for, otherwise children and families pay the cost. This paper describes the model of assessment and matching used by Barnardo's Family Placement Services. If reflects 12 years of practice experience as an agency specialising in the placement of children with "special needs". There are three key elements to the model:

1) Agree the broad package of care based on an accurate assessment of the child's needs. This includes basis of placement, essential requirements of families and the support needed.
2) Tailor this package to the individual child – based on knowledge gained through direct work with the child.
3) Empower families to parent the child.

Assessment of the child

The importance of a multidisciplinary assessment of a child's needs prior to placement is increasingly being recognised. A comprehensive assessment must include a child's education and medical needs. The adoption agency's responsibility is to build onto the above a component describing the child's needs as they are likely to impact on a family.

In building this picture, one of the tools Family Placement Services uses is the Project's "Child Assessment Form". This was developed by McKenna and Cairns[1] and draws extensively on the work of Fahlberg.[2] It serves as a checklist and covers various areas of the child's functioning, eg. physical, social, emotional, sexual development, and attachment capacity. Questions are also structured around the carers' experience of looking after the child. Information collated by completing the questionnaire with current foster carers and, where possible, previous carers, is then taken together with what is known about the child's early history and behaviour patterns evidenced at home or during previous placements. A comprehensive picture is built up which allows workers to measure the child's past/present functioning and place them on a continuum of having more or less difficulties in different areas. The complexity of the child's needs can then be broadly categorised as indicating low, medium or high risk, with subsequent implications for the basis of placement, the qualities looked for in families, and the support package required.

Two case examples will help illustrate how this works in practice.

Alan

Alan was nine years old when referred to the Project for adoption. His early life was characterised by disruption: alcohol abuse, marital discord and violence were all features of his parents' lifestyle. Alan was the subject of both physical and sexual abuse, and was admitted to care when he was six years old. Two foster placements disrupted as a result of Alan's aggressive behaviour, and carers also felt very uncomfortable with his sexualised behaviour. Alan was admitted to a Children's Unit. His need for therapeutic help was identified and met. He made excellent use of therapy sessions to begin to act out some of his abusive experiences, and express some of his anger and confusion. The Child Assessment report prepared at the time of referral indicated a child who retained some very significant problems, aggressive behaviour, temper tantrums and inappropriate sexual behaviour towards women. Significantly he was also a child who carers felt very warmly towards and who did form attachments. He made positive relationships both with his therapist and his key worker in the Children's Unit. There was also evidence that through these relationships he was beginning to be able to modify his behaviour.

Alan's placement was acknowledged as being a medium/high risk placement. In the preparation and planning for Alan's adoptive placement it was clear that any adoptive family was going to need considerable support. In conjunction with the local authority a support package was planned and agreed prior to any introductions to prospective adopters; the local authority would continue to pay a fee to Family Placement Services for providing the following post-adoption support:

- individual casework support for as long as was required;
- access to support groups;
- access to training:
  - "reparenting the sexually abused child"
  - " handling difficult behaviour"
  - "safe restraint techniques"
- respite care if requested.

Alan would continue to receive individual therapy for at least one year into placement, after which Alan's therapist would offer consultancy to Alan's adoptive family. It was vital that all of these elements were agreed *prior* to placement. They have proved essential in sustaining what has been an extremely challenging adoptive placement.

Stuart

Stuart was referred to the Project for permanency at age ten. The "care" Stuart experienced in his early life was at best neglectful, at worst abusive. Alcohol abuse, mental health problems, marital discord and violence were all features of his parents' lifestyle. Stuart had numerous placements in institutional care, followed by three foster placements, all of which were intended to be permanent but all of which disrupted. Stuart's behaviour in all the placements was extremely difficult. At the time of undertaking the assessment Stuart was placed in a specialist fostering scheme. There was a remarkable degree of congruence between descriptions of Stuart in previous placements and in this placement. Recurrent themes that emerged were "coldness", "superficiality", "lack of genuineness", "lack of guilt and remorse", "indiscriminately affectionate", "constant lying", "cruelty to animals" and "preoccupation with blood, fire and gore". Various carers described feelings of "exasperation", "anger" and "hopelessness". Superficially, however, Stuart was charming and engaging and an adoptive family came forward for him. The Project and the local authority took the risk in placing Stuart. Sadly, but perhaps predictably, the placement disrupted 15 months after Stuart was placed. The warning signs were very clear – extreme early adversity and a history of severe emotional and behavioural problems that had not ameliorated over time despite good quality care.

The support package provided proved singularly ineffective in preventing the breakdown of Stuart's placement. This is consistent with research findings that models of empowerment, and traditional insight therapy, are not sufficient to achieve positive outcomes for children with such severe and entrenched negative behaviour patterns.[3,4,5]

Learning from the US experience

In the USA, Stuart's symptoms would have labelled him as a child with "reactive attachment disorder" which is described in greater detail in Section III. While we might question the usefulness of labelling children, the acknowledgement of the "condition" in the USA has led to the development of more radical therapeutic treatment such as "holding therapy". Cline[6] argues that traditional insight directed therapeutic approaches are not successful with children with severe attachment difficulties. Instead therapy must be designed to help the child repeat early experiences this time with a successful outcome. This helps the child develop a basic sense of trust. Rage reduction or holding therapy is designed to force the child through an arousal/relaxation cycle – the process by which babies normally develop trust.

Figure 1
Holding therapy

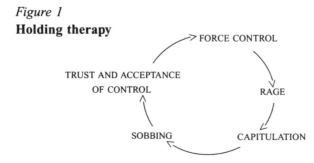

A therapist confronted with the vast extent of the child's anger and panic needs to be able to act as a "safe container" for all these angry, hostile feelings. It is not surprising that adoptive families can feel overwhelmed when confronted with similar displays of the depths of the children's anger and despair. Cline's base, The Attachment Centre at Evergreen, USA, offers a variety of support packages to adoptive families. Parents are offered a two week long intensive programme where child and parents are worked with individually and together. Holding therapy may be a component of work with the child, and the parent is included in this when the child is ready to "bond". Parents are also shown behaviour management techniques.

In other situations the child's difficulties are so severe, and the parents so alienated from the child, that a large period of out of home treatment is recommended. The child in this situation would live with one of the Attachment Centre's therapeutic foster families and receive therapy at the Centre. A high measure of success is reported in being able to subsequently restore children to their adoptive families.

As children move through the continuum of "low risk" to "high risk", the demands placed on families seeking to parent them increase. The more complex the child's needs, the greater the additional qualities and skills that will be required from our carers. "High risk" children do not allow parents normal parental narcissism; satisfactions have to come from different sources.

Equally, as adoption agencies, if we are to help children like Stuart and his adoptive family, then we need to learn from the US experience and develop a similar range of more radical approaches. All of the above can be summarised diagrammatically (see the following page).

Tailoring the package to the individual child

Having ensured that the basic support package is right, what is then needed is to fine tune this package to the individual child's needs. Undertaking direct work with children provides the opportunity to ascertain answers to questions like – where do his/her attachments lie? Which ongoing contacts should be maintained? What is the child's sense of identity, sense of his or her past? What work might be needed to enhance this child's self esteem? What feelings lie behind the behaviours? What

	Low risk/complexity	Medium risk/complexity	High risk/complexity
Child factors	Good enough early parenting. Not too extreme behaviour. Evidence of capacity to form good attachments and grow and develop. Child under 10	Poor early parenting. Significant behaviour problems. More limited capacity to form attachments and modify behaviour. Child under 10	Very poor early parenting. Severe behavioural problems. Persistence of these problems over time, despite sensitive caring. Lack of attachment. Child 10+ on placement
Basis of placement	Adoption	Fostering/adoption	Fostering/residential treatment
Essential qualities required by families	Relevant experience/evidence of understanding child's needs. Ability to use support. Acceptance of difference in foster/adoptive parenting. Safe caring.	As low risk plus: flexibility and ability and willingness to adjust expectations of the child. Ability to find satisfaction in small increments of improvement.	As before plus perseverance, commitment, sense of humour and tolerance of child's rejection. Ability to delay gratification.
Support package required	Adoption allowance. Access to social work support as needed. Appropriate specialist help. Access to support group. Access to ongoing training, eg. behavioural management techniques. Active involvement from adoption agency may not be required for long periods of time. Support reactivated at key transitions, eg. adolescence. Reunion with birth parents.	As low risk plus: specific specialist help, eg. in education. Respite care. Therapy. Mediation re: openess.	Carers as key elements of support in package of care that may involve respite, therapy and residential treatment.

is the child's need for and readiness to engage in therapeutic work?

The Project has found books such as *Direct Work with Children*[7] and *Communicating through Play*[8] as well as various children's books, helpful in structuring our work with children. The following case extracts highlight some of what we can learn by communicating with and listening to children.

In deciding the degree of openness it is important to establish the level of attachment to the birth family and the meaning of access for the child. For some children, although the quality of access may not seem that great, nevertheless it is an important constant in the child's life.

> *In terms of future paths David did not construct one that involved living with or sharing with Dad. Instead Dad's visits were mentioned as something that would continue to happen; David ranked these exactly halfway in a list of 10 future paths. I had a very strong sense from David as he did these exercises that his relationship with Dad is an important constant in his life, which nevertheless is limited in what it can offer him. This may well be how access visits are experienced.*

The child's sense of identity and view of him or herself can also be tested out. For a black child the experience of racism and perception of the self as black will be particularly important. John is of mixed parentage.

> *Of great significance for his own black identity is, I think, the fact that he chose a mixed parentage lady as being the most attractive person out of a selection of pictures I had i.e. notably more attractive than a white lady . . . I believe that although John is not denying culture, work does need to be done to build and expand on his understanding and experience of "colour".*

Particular work that might help with this can then be identified. In John's case, a decision was taken to recruit a black befriender as part of a support package for him.

Incorporating the child's perspective into the assessment can also help identify the positive survival function that some behaviours have for a child.

> *John knows and accepts racism as a fact, but he is not willing*

> *simply to tolerate it and will use a variety of methods to combat it*
> *actively. John does have an "arrogance" in his personality which*
> *some people may find disturbing, but it is a good defence*
> *mechanism for his situation at present.*

Listening to the child helps us convey to families the reasons behind the child's difficult presenting behaviour. This is the beginning of helping adoptive families empathise with a child's situation, a quality that will be essential if adoptive families are to be able to stick with the child.

> *David's anger and resentment which he brought to the sessions*
> *enabled me to explore a little with him the nature of his anger.*
> *David was able to say how he couldn't be as angry as he really*
> *felt because otherwise he would just "destroy everything". Again*
> *there is a real tension for David between his fear and the power*
> *of his destructive fantasies. The only expression David can find*
> *under this tension is through his sullen, resentful behaviour.*
> *Ripping bits of wallpaper when he feels like "breaking up the*
> *whole bedroom" reflects the impotence David feels about making*
> *sense of or influencing his life.*

The way in which a child uses these sessions also helps us assess the child's need for and capacity to engage in more sustained therapeutic work. It may identify a particular area of work that project staff could undertake, eg. work that helps the child separate out feelings about their birth family and/or new adoptive family, or work that builds on previous life story work to incorporate a child's increased level of understanding about the past. In adolescence, identity issues are likely to resurface and additional help may be required at this stage. The project worker may have an important mediating role to play in the re-establishment of contact with the birth family. Periods of intensive involvement directly with the child may be followed by lengthy periods of very low key involvement. Work can be re-activated at critical stages for the child. Adolescents may welcome the opportunity of being part of a peer group of adopted adolescents thus helping lessen their sense of difference and isolation. Whilst we may be able to identify some elements of the direct work with a child prior to placement, some needs may not emerge until much later. As agencies we need to be able to respond flexibly.

Assessment and preparation of adopters

By this stage we have a clear picture of the child's overall functioning, and his or her particular needs; what is now required is to put families in as strong a position as we can to meet these needs. We need to evolve our practice by listening to what families find most helpful.

General approach

Family Placement Services structures preparation, assessment and training for families in the following way. We begin with three introductory sessions designed to help carers understand the unique aspects of foster/adoptive parenting, and help them decide whether this is right for them. Assessment work then begins. At a later stage families have modular sessions including ones on attachment, separation and loss, and an introductory one on the impact of child sexual abuse. This structure was arrived at following an in-house evaluation of our preparation and training.[9] The clear message received was that applicants' anxiety pre-approval hindered them from taking in much information.

Systemic assessment

The Project's assessment now uses a systemic assessment which involves work with the whole family.

A growing frustration with traditional family assessment which focused on past history, coupled with a belief that it was more important to look at a family's current functioning, led to the introduction of a systemic approach to family assessment. The format for systemic assessment has been two workers sharing the role of interviewer/observer. A minimum of three interviews involving the whole family are held in the office. Topics covered include the decision to foster/adopt, the impact on each family member, family tree, aspects of family functioning/roles, parenting, time/space, managing stress and safe caring. Other areas have been added as required. Workers have identified many strengths to this approach. The heart of the application and key issues were more readily reached, leading to quicker and sharper assessments. There was a clarity of dynamics in working with the whole family, i.e. seeing patterns of interaction. The richness of working with what happens, not just what is said, provided another level of evidence for assessment. The children's input was particularly useful in understanding how a child is likely to experience a particular family. Families who have been assessed by traditional methods, and then assessed using a systemic approach for a subsequent application, have commented positively on the approach.

> *The group meetings were very carefully timed, this being a much shorter time than normal assessments and the children seemed to enjoy being able to participate.*

> *On the whole I found this assessment to be very organised and time saving as opposed to the other methods of assessment – it was quite a searching process but at the end I felt a very insightful report was produced.*

Families have also been able to see an obvious connection between the topic covered and having a child placed with them. A connection that has not always been so easily grasped when focusing on events that happened to prospective adopters 20, 30 or even 40 years previously!

Applicants attending panel

Another important practice development has been to invite applicants to attend at their Approval Panel – this has been the Project's practice since 1988. Inviting applicants to attend the Panel is consistent with, and reinforces, the principle of partnership between adoptive parents and the Project. It empowers applicants, and promotes self advocacy qualities which we know to be important in successful family placements for children with "special needs". The practice has been evaluated from the perspective of panel members, project workers and applicants, with benefits to all parties being identified. Applicants who have attended have found the experience nerve-wracking but useful.

> *We wanted to be fully part of the decision making process.*

> *I wanted to explain my own feelings in person.*

Preparation of family for individual child

The Child Assessment report gives a detailed picture of the child's behaviour, and it is essential that this full information is then shared with prospective carers. This then allows for very specific preparation of families, for the behaviour they might expect, and the opportunity to rehearse strategies for managing it. We have learned from feedback from our adoptive parents that both the timing of such work and the content are important.

> *It is important for adopters to know not just what type of behaviour to expect, but also how they might "feel", faced with a real live situation . . . We did not explore what we would actually feel if a child punched us and swore at us in the middle of a local shopping centre at peak time, or in front of our mother or church minister. I suggest the time for undertaking this deeper work is not at the pre-assessment groups, but after adoptive parents have been approved.*[10]

Another task is to start the process of bonding by creating empathy for the child's situation. The sharing of the information from our direct work with children helps achieve this. It puts adoptive parents in touch with the vulnerabilities and needs of the child that lie behind the presenting behaviour. Barnardo's New Families Newcastle hold a "Life Appreciation Day for the Child", post-approval of the match but pre-placement. Adopters have found this a very powerful way of getting in touch with their child's experience to date. Keeping carers in touch with the "inner child" is essential if they are to be sustained through what will undoubtedly be difficult and testing times ahead.

Post-placement training

No amount of preparation and training pre-placement can adequately prepare families for the reality of living with the child. What we need to ensure is that access to more in-depth training is available to families post-placement as needed.

Family Placement Services, in conjunction with our associate project, Scottish Adoption Advice Service, offers a range of workshop/training events. These evolve and remain responsive to needs expressed by adopters. There are nevertheless certain key themes that re-emerge so frequently that they are now fixed entities in our annual training programme. A "Telling Workshop" is held on how to tell children that they are adopted and how to share with them difficult background information. Openness and contact is another general theme that adopters often value the opportunity to explore, both in relation to their own and their child's feelings about "belonging" to two family systems. All children placed for adoption have experienced separation and loss. The vast majority of children placed by Family Placement Services have been neglected, abused emotionally, physically and/or sexually. It is not surprising that this experience is then reflected in difficult behaviour. The project runs two training sessions on handling difficult behaviour, one which focuses on primary school children, and the other on adolescents. Common behavioural problems in adopted children, such as lying and stealing, are explored in depth. Explicit acknowledgement is given to the additional tasks that face children who are separated from their family of origin. Parenting children who have been sexually abused is another course which is repeated annually; safe caring practices are also explored as well as strategies for managing sexually inappropriate behaviour.

Systemic post-placement support
The project is only beginning to explore the potential benefits of using a systemic model post-placement. Already, however, we are becoming aware of some of the strengths of this approach. In one situation, post-adoption support had been offered by a casework model for the previous six years. The adopted person (now 17) clearly identified the project worker as being his parents' worker. It was also hard for both the adopters and the project worker to look at the problems with any kind of freshness. A series of three systemic interviews, conducted jointly with a new Family Placement Services worker and a local authority worker, achieved a remarkable degree of progress in helping this family acknowledge some of the positives in their situation, and agree strategies about living with each other. The benefits of the increased structure and focus do seem to carry on into post-placement support.

The next stage for the Project will be to use a systemic approach at an earlier stage to assist both the child and family in forming attachments.

A model for this is provided by Beech Brook Spaulding Adoption Programme, Cleveland, USA, with their "Family Bonding Programme" that is offered to all families who take placements of older children. Different "bonding strategies" are linked to what are identified as four phases in the attachment process:

- *The Honeymoon Phase* where the child is actually unattached and his/her behaviour reflects little or no emotional involvement;
- *The Ambivalent Phase* where the model behaviour disappears and the child begins to test the family to see if he/she is accepted as a family member – not only when he/she behaves well but also when he/she acts out. The family at this stage also faces ambivalent feelings.
- *The Reciprocal Interaction Phase*: A successful resolution of phase two results in the family "letting go" of their "ideal child" and beginning to establish a mutually satisfying relationship with the child. This phase, called the Reciprocal Interaction Phase, lays the foundation for Phase four.
- *Bond Solidification*: A variety of tools such as lifestory books, life maps, famegraphs, family sculptures, and disclosure exercises are used at different stages to assist the development of attachment.[11] This would seem a very natural extension of the work begun in the systemic assessment.

Conclusion

This paper describes a model of assessment and matching. It identifies a framework for assessing risk and tailoring our placement package around the child's needs. Our work with adoptive parents should be about equipping and empowering them to parent the child. All of the above should ensure that a placement gets off to the best possible start. It is only the beginning!

References

1. McKenna M, and Cairns V, *Barnardo's Child Assessment Form*, Family Placement Services, Edinburgh, 1990.

2. Fahlberg V, *A Child's Journey through Placement*, BAAF, 1994.

3. Thoburn J, *Success and Failure in Permanent Family Placement*, Ashgate Publishing, 1990.

4. Borland M, et al, *Permenancy Planning for Children in Lothian Region*, 1989.

5. Rushton A, Treseder J, and Quinton D, *New Parents for Older Children*, BAAF, 1988.

6. Cline F, *Understanding and Treating the Severely Disturbed Child*, Evergreen Consultants in Human Behaviour, 1979, USA.

7. Aldgate J, and Simmons J (eds), *Direct Work with Children – A guide for social work practitioners*, BAAF/Batsford, 1988.

8. Cipolla J, Benson McGown D, and Yanulis M A, *Communicating through Play – Techniques for assessing and preparing children for adoption*, BAAF, 1992.

9. MacFadyen S, *Preparing or Deterring? Consumer feedback on preparation groups for prospective adopters in Barnardo's Family Placement Services Project* in Fuller R, and Petch A, *Practitioner Research*, Open University Press, 1995.

10. Munro C, *The Child Within*, The Children's Society, 1993.

11. Hughes, and Rosenberg, *Family Bonding with High Risks Placements*, Halworth Press, 1990.

2 The use of adoption allowances to sustain adoption placements

Emma McWilliam

Emma McWilliam is Professional Officer, Adoption and Fostering, Central Region Social Work Services.

Adoption allowances were initially introduced in order to secure adoption placements for "hard to place" children such as sibling groups, older children and children with severe disabilities. It was envisaged that adoption allowances would be paid in a minority of cases. However, as the number of infants being adopted steadily declines, the majority of children placed for adoption in the 1990s have special needs. Adoption Allowance Regulations were introduced in England and Wales in 1991 and the indications are that Scotland is likely to follow suit as part of the Children (Scotland) Act 1995. Unfortunately, the existing Regulations make no overall statement about the intended purpose of adoption allowances.

Most authorities make a decision about whether to pay adoption allowances at an adoption panel, either when registering a child for adoption, or matching a child with a prospective adoptive family. Often the decision is based on "market forces", that is, the likelihood of finding an adoptive placement without paying allowances, instead of an assessment of the child's long-term needs and the financial implications for adopters attempting to meet these. Making a decision about adoption allowances at one point in time denies the fact that many significant changes can occur over the duration of an adoption placement. These may be in terms of the needs of the child or the circumstances of the adoptive family. For example, if an adopted child in a closed adoption later on has contact with members of his/her birth family, the practicalities of such arrangements in terms of travel, accommodation, etc. can be costly. Adoptive families who become claimants of Income Support find that their adoption allowances are treated as income and reduce their entitlement to benefit, thus penalising the poorest adoptive families.

A significant reduction in an adoptive family's income may have a detrimental effect on the kind of compensatory experiences a child can be given, or jeopardise the actual placement. For example, I worked with a couple who adopted two older emotionally damaged sisters. Three years into placement the adoptive mother died. Adoption allowances were provided by the placing authority to enable the adoptive father to give up his work and care for the children on a full-time basis. The solution to such problems is for authorities to take a long-term flexible approach. In cases where adoption allowances are not approved at the start of a placement, there should be the option of activating these at a later date if necessary. This may have the added benefit of targeting adoption allowances at adoptive families during particular periods of need, rather than panel members feeling that they have to safeguard adopters from the outset of a placement in anticipation of what may occur later on.

Some financially hard pressed authorities are changing their annual review procedures with the aim of making savings in their ongoing adoption allowance budgets. Situations have arisen, for example, in the placements of large sibling groups, where proposals have been made to reduce the original amount of adoption allowances in response to the children doing well in placement and presenting fewer problems. It can be imagined that this has not found favour with the adoptive parents as a reward for their efforts.

Adoption allowance schemes must be explicit and all adoptive parents should receive written information about how these will be operated. Adoption allowances are not an area in which to look for savings, as adoption represents the best value for money compared to all other forms of child care provision. In fact, publicity about adoption allowances should be more prominent in adoption recruitment campaigns as many people still rule themselves out of coming forward in the belief that they cannot afford to adopt. Reducing the time that children in the care system wait before an adoptive family can be found decreases the risk of placement disruption, with the likely long-term consequence of more expensive forms of child care provision. It has been suggested that adoption allowances should be "tagged" automatically to some children at the point of registration for adoption as a means of ensuring their prospects of placement, and that the allowance would come with the child regardless of the financial circumstances of the prospective adoptive family. A more fundamental question is whether all adopted children should have a right to an adoption allowance on the grounds that any child who has been accommodated is, by definition, a "child in need".[1]

Professionals involved in post-adoption support work often find themselves identifying resources which are required to sustain placements but for which funding is not readily available, for example, therapeutic help for the child, counselling for adoptive parents, respite facilities, educational supports and training opportunities. One possible means of financing such resources is for adoptive parents to be able to pay for these directly themselves by using their adoption allowances. It can be argued that such a solution empowers adoptive parents by giving them control as purchasers of appropriate services.

I have had recent experiences of this approach to obtaining post-adoption support services for some adoptive families.

Robin

One childless couple had a three-year-old boy, Robin, placed with them for adoption; Robin was thought to be a relatively straightforward child at the point of matching, and therefore adoption allowances were not approved. By the time Robin was nine, the adopters requested a psychological assessment due to his increasing emotional and behavioural difficulties. The psychologist was of the opinion that Robin was experiencing serious long-term problems relating to his early childhood experiences such as a lack of attachment, severe neglect and possible abuse. The recommendation was that he receive psychotherapy twice weekly for at least two years, and that the adoptive parents would need the support of another therapist for themselves while this was taking place. Neither the Health Board nor the Education Department could provide this service, or the funding to purchase it from an alternative source. The adoptive parents therefore approached the placing adoption agency and requested that adoption allowances be initiated for as long as this therapeutic intervention was necessary. The amount of the weekly adoption allowance was almost equivalent to the weekly costs they would incur to pay for this service, a suitable resource having been identified. The placing agency agreed to this arrangement with some reluctance, because of the budgetary implications and ambiguity about their responsibility towards the family. Because of where the adoptive parents lived, if the placement disrupted, the child would have been received into the care of a different local authority than the one from which he had been placed. This expenditure could therefore not be viewed by the authority who had placed the child as a preventive measure to save greater expense in the long term.

In another case, an adoptive family was already receiving an adoption allowance for their ten-year-old daughter, Helen.

Helen

Helen's adoptive family had previously fostered her and her younger brother and adoption allowances had been awarded to enable them to afford to proceed to adopt the two children. Helen was displaying increasingly sexualised behaviour, soiling and wetting and appeared to have many issues to work through in relation to her birth family. The school psychologist was of the opinion that she would benefit from art therapy as she had great difficulty in expressing her feelings. The only suitable resource was a self-employed therapist, but there was no funding available. The placing adoption agency therefore agreed to enhance the existing adoption allowance for the duration of the treatment so that the adoptive parents could afford to pay for this help. In this instance, the placement was in the same authority from which the children originated. There were stronger arguments for financial investment to strengthen the placement in order to reduce the risk of disruption in adolescence, and the possible consequent long-term costs of residential care.

These two examples raise several questions in relation to how the costs of post-adoption support services are to be met and who has responsibility for doing so. The use of an adoption allowance to assist in obtaining adoption placements for children cannot be seen as an end in itself. There must be recognition that where children have been emotionally damaged, further expenditure may be necessary in order to sustain placements. The more creative use of adoption allowances may provide a solution in some situations and I would like to see the Social Services Inspectorate acting as a positive influence on this issue. Sadly, without such a lead, local authorities, in the current financial climate, are in danger of interpreting their adoption allowance schemes in an ever more restrictive manner.

References

1. Hughes B, *Post Placement Services for Children and Families: Defining the need*, Department of Health, Social Services Inspectorate, 1995.

3 Special needs at school

Paul Dumbleton

Paul Dumbleton is an adoptive parent.

Children with special needs bring a lot of hard work with them. The "special" in the term "special needs" means that the child needs extra support over and above the support all children need: extra visits to hospital, extra visits from the health visitor, extra professionals in your life, extra worry about which school to choose or which school will accept your child. Despite this no one ever asks us why we wanted to adopt a child with special needs. Perhaps the question never occurs to them, but it seems more likely that it is the sort of question that they are simply too polite to ask. Why choose to bring all that on yourself, especially as, in our case, we have two perfectly happy and healthy birth children already?

I do not have an answer. Both Sue, my wife, and I worked with people with disabilities. At the time we adopted our daughter, Lyn, I worked in special education in a further education college, and Sue worked for a housing association providing supported housing for people with learning disabilities. I suppose we felt we knew something about the right and wrong way to treat people with disabilities and that we could make a better job of things than most. Even the social worker who assessed our suitability as adopters often said, 'You know more about this than I do'. It was flattering and at the time seemed reassuring, but it simply meant that she felt that our professional expertise equipped us to parent a child with special needs. Her confidence did not, however, prepare us for the experience of parenting a child with special needs and nor did any of the assessment or pre-placement activities. For while we were expected to visit children's homes and day nurseries, we were not offered the chance to speak to other adoptive parents of children with special needs. Although professionals often say that parents are the real experts, this was not reflected in our assessment or preparation for adoption.

The world of special needs is populated by large numbers of professionals and the fact that we were a part of that world seemed to count in our favour with those considering our application. To them it meant, at least, that we were realistic in our expectations.

This would seem a reasonable assumption to anyone but the parent of a child with special needs, who would quickly tell you that most professionals have little insight into the home life of children with special needs and that many, apparently, have little interest. They are interested in *an aspect* of the child, but few seem to want to know about the child herself rather than the particular aspect that interests them. Of course there are some wonderful health visitors, teachers and doctors but there are some terrible ones as well. Lyn has a great speech therapist but a previous one discharged her as beyond the help of speech therapy. The good ones seem to be good because of who they are, not because of their professional training or expertise. In fact some forms of training seem to encourage a sort of detached arrogance towards children and their parents above which only the best individuals can rise.

Of course our work in the field of special needs cannot offer any real explanation of our decision to adopt a child with special needs. It simply begs the questions of why we work in that field. But whatever the reasons, we felt we had room in our family for another child and, six years ago, Lyn moved in with us and was duly adopted the following year. She was three years old and had lived in the same temporary foster home for most of her life.

Her developmental delay had been recognised at an early stage but the degree to which this was caused by her poor early environment, or was due to inherent factors, was never clear. By the time she came to live with us she already had a weekly session with a pre-school home teacher having been assessed by an educational psychologist as being unlikely to cope other than in a special school. Apart from generally delayed development she was also very reluctant to speak to almost all adults, although she talked to us immediately and, within the home, appeared to adapt very quickly to her new life with us. She has remained reluctant to speak to adults and although she quickly gets used to some, she steadfastly refuses to speak to others. This can be embarrassing for us and disconcerting for them if they work with her.

Experiences with the education department

School is a very big part of any child's life. In some ways it is even more important to children with special needs as it is also the place where other services are delivered and the place which aims to help overcome the difficulties that cause the special needs. Our experiences of school, or more accurately, the services of the Education Department, have not been altogether happy. This is not because Lyn goes to a bad school, or has uncaring teachers. In fact the difficulties we have experienced with staff of the Education Department seem to increase in inverse proportion to the person's degree of direct contact with Lyn. Supervisory assistants and classroom teachers are kind to her and have some insight into her wider life. But such a child comes into contact with, and brings her parents into contact with, the bureaucracy of the Education Department through the Record of Needs procedure. This means, at least, contact with a headteacher, an educational psychologist and a doctor. As we have found ourselves in disagreement with these weighty professionals we have also had to work with senior staff of various branches of the Education Department. As we moved further away from the classroom and closer to the decision makers, Lyn's needs seemed not only more remote but of increasingly less importance compared to policy, finance and a measure of ideology. For the world of special needs is full of powerful ideologies regarding the rights and wrongs of, for example, integration into mainstream schools. These make fascinating debates for professionals, but can get in the way of helping individual children.

There are a number of problems which, as people familiar with this system, we could have anticipated but did not. The most obvious of these is the lack of information available to parents. It is not possible to make informed decisions, or contribute to discussion and planning, without information on what is available and the processes that are necessary to access various services.

The Education Department of the area in which we live provides no information on its special educational or psychological services. For some time it even withheld the Scottish Office publication for parents with special needs as a matter of official policy! For three years enquiries about the availability of general information on special educational services elicited replies about leaflets "in preparation" but never actually elicited an information leaflet. On more than one occasion, through good luck or hard work, we have discovered services which would benefit our daughter. Each time the service has, eventually, been added to her record, but we are left wondering if there are other, undiscovered services about which we know nothing.

This would not be of such a great concern if it were not for the second major difficulty – the lack of a consistent approach by professional services, for example, educational psychologists, the key "gate keepers" to most special educational services. Our daughter has had a number of psychologists who operate in very different ways. Psychologists are very keen to defend their individual professional judgement which effectively means that different psychologists seem to be doing quite different jobs and tell you different things. One may tell you about, and even recommend, a course of action that another does not even consider worth mentioning. This would be less worrying if parents had all the relevant information to hand, but they have to rely on the filter of the judgement of a psychologist for this information.

A third major difficulty which we could have foreseen but did not was the effort of dealing with the bureaucracy of the Record of Needs and all the other professional services with which parents of children with special needs come into contact. This takes time even if things are going well, but can become an exhausting burden if parents have to disagree with professionals and fight for services for their children. While service providers now consult parents, the willingness to consult does not usually extend as far as a willingness to consult at a time determined by parents, or to provide creche or other facilities. The lack of information for parents makes preparation for such meetings very time consuming in itself. While it is now fashionable for professionals who work with children with special needs to say that they believe in partnership with parents, many seem to have changed only superficially.

Including parents in decision making is not an easy option and requires planning and careful thought about how best to facilitate parental involvement and how professional roles will be modified by this. Most professionals do not seem really willing to share decision making with families, unless the family always agrees with them.

Acknowledging differences and difficulties

We could have foreseen these and other difficulties if we had thought more about our working lives, but there is one major difficulty that we could not have foreseen because we were, in a sense, a part of the problem. We shared the current professional perspective which dictates that the positive aspects of a child's abilities are stressed and the child's difficulties or disabilities are not emphasised. There are very good reasons for this. It is all too easy to speak of "the disabled" as a special group or even separate species. It is all too easy to present children with special needs as the objects of charity rather than as participants in and contributors to society. But it is also all too easy to forget the emotional difficulties which face a child who cannot do what his or her peers can do, and the pain of parents who see their child struggling.

Simply deciding that we do not call children "handicapped" or "disabled" any more and that we want to take a positive view of things does not do away with the difficulties that they face. Of course we should assert that all children are the same, but only in the sense that they are of equal worth and, for example, deserve to be treated with respect, loved and given the opportunity to learn. We would be fooling ourselves if we did not recognise that in other important ways children are all different, and that some are "more different" than others. It is now fashionable to say that all children are special, but this can easily distract attention away from the individual child with particular difficulties. The professional optimism and positive view of special needs has been developed to counter previous, negative perspectives, but perhaps also because it is not comfortable to think about other people's pain. Of course we need positive attitudes and actions and the best teaching and equipment but, for my daughter, it is still hard to see, to learn and to make relationships. A sense of pain of living with those differences often seems missing from the current, positive professional perspective, which seems keen to recognise her similarities to most children but reluctant to acknowledge her difficulties.

Lessons for adoption workers

My experience of Lyn's education probably reflects more strongly the fact that she has special needs than that she is adopted. The families which we feel we have most in common with are families which include a child with special needs rather than those who have an adopted child. But, of course, a significant proportion of adopted children have disabilities or learning difficulties, and many others face problems at school because of emotional difficulties which manifest themselves as difficult behaviour. So, what are the lessons for professionals in adoption services?

Firstly, there is a real need for good preparation for adoptive families, and this must include contact with other families of children with special needs. If professionals believe that parents are the real experts this should be reflected in preparation for adoption. After adoption, parents of children with special needs need continuing support as do all adoptive parents from time to time. But they also need support because they are parents of children with special needs. Even in the best of situations almost all parents of children with special needs report that they have to take on the weight of professional bureaucracy to get a fair deal for their children. This reflects not only the inevitable differences between individuals, but the fact that "special" needs are needs over and above those of other children. As there seems no prospect of an easing of the current restrictions on public budgets, there will be inevitable conflicts between parents' perceptions of their children's needs, and the needs that authorities are prepared to recognise and meet.

Parents need practical supports of all sorts, for example, it can be difficult to get baby-sitters for children with special needs, and many such children are socially isolated and need organised play opportunities. But in relation to the education system, parents need the moral support of an experienced post-adoption support worker who trusts their judgement of the best interests of their child, and who can discuss educational opportunities and options without any interest in the potential cost to the authority. This could be extended to advocacy of support for parents by joining them at meetings with education professionals.

A significant proportion of the hard work that children with special needs bring with them is the struggle of dealing with the child's education. Adoption authorities should be aware of this and be prepared to support parents, so that they can get on with being parents rather than campaigners on behalf of their children.

4   Adopted children in mainstream education
A personal experience

Elaine Ainslie

Elaine Ainslie is an adoptive parent and Chairperson of the Lothian Adopters Group (LAG).

It is amazing, when a group of adoptive parents get together, how quickly the conversation turns to the subject of education in all its aspects. Adoptive parents often have problems with the education system, but do not know what their children are entitled to, or how to get help.

We have three adopted children. Two brothers, Mark and Andy, who were placed thirteen years ago, aged six and five years respectively. Zoe was placed eleven years ago, aged fifteen months. The boys had been in care for two and a half years prior to placement with us. In that time, they had had twelve homes, sometimes together, and fifteen months of it was spent in a children's home. A chequered start!

Mark

Mark, our eldest, went straight into a primary 1 class on placement. He was a bright child and settled in well and made friends. However, he was easily distracted and needed to be kept an eye on as he was the class clown. His teachers had been sympathetic to his background – too sympathetic at times. Mark knew how to manipulate them – he had learnt how adults "work" whilst he was in care. The school did not discourage my visits to the classroom and readily communicated any problems or concerns.

Once Mark was in secondary school I made an appointment to see the Year 1 Head teacher as I foresaw difficulties with Mark as he grew older. I explained that Mark needed to be monitored closely and we would appreciate co-operation from the school, if difficulties arose, in communicating such problems to us. We would, of course, back up the school and help to try and sort out problems. I had in the past done some voluntary teaching in the school and was well known to the year Head. I contacted her at the start of each term. She listened to me, but I left feeling I had been classed as an over-anxious parent.

At the end of the first year, the school report came in. In traditional style, it was a page per subject. In every subject except PE and art there were comments about Mark's lack of concentration. I asked the Year Head for Mark to be referred to the educational psychologist; although she could not see that there was a problem, she agreed to do so. The letter that went to the Education Department said, 'Mark's mother wants him referred'. We had dealt with the psychologist before as he had tested Andy. He expressed surprise that the school did not perceive any difficulties. He identified that Mark was of above average intelligence, but that he had problems with concentration due to an overriding preoccupation with his birth family. He also thought Mark was a child who liked the excitement of the moment without considering the consequences.

At parents' evening we talked to every teacher about Mark's difficulties. Some were surprised to hear of Mark's adoption and felt it explained a lot. None of the information I had given to the year Head had been passed on. We asked each teacher to inform us if his homework was not done or if there was a problem. Most said they could not as they would have to refer it up the management line to the year Head; it would be up to her to do something. We explained we were more than happy for them to telephone us directly, but only one took us up on it.

Over the next school year several things happened in the boys' lives. Their natural family turned up on our doorstep. This completely threw Mark, which resulted in difficult behaviour and some police involvement. I kept the school informed. I still felt I was being patted on the back and told not to be over-anxious. Then year 3 began and Mark started to miss school, get into trouble, and his work slipped. It would be fair to say the school wrote him off at this stage. He obviously was not doing much in class and they did not give homework to the lower groups. The reason given was it was not worth it (the logic of this still escapes me!). We were suddenly being blamed for Mark's behaviour. We had talked to the staff at school for two years saying there would be problems and had been told not to be silly, and yet when problems arose, they were now perceived to be our fault!

Life at home was becoming more difficult and it was affecting the other children. So between the educational psychologist, the social worker, the Children's Hearing Panel and ourselves, it was decided that Mark needed residential schooling. In the meantime I was often up at the school – there was no problem in phoning us regularly now! On one of the last occasions I was taken up to the headmaster's office. I think he expected to tick me off and end his interview in ten minutes. In fact it lasted an hour. He ended his "speech" saying they had done everything they could for Mark and there was nothing more they could try. I was angry and explained that I had communicated with the school from the first weeks but this positive resource had not been used. He replied that he was not aware of this but would look into it. I never heard from him again!

We now had a new educational psychologist as the previous one had been promoted. She suggested we look at various schools for Mark, to see which one suited him best. We looked at the Region's residential school, a special day school unit, and residential school in the next county, Fife. The third school was the best, in our opinion, as it was small and homely, and had a psychologist attached to it who was the only one who ran a clinic for adopted children in Scotland. (This clinic is not in existence any longer.) Mark had seen him previously at his clinic. It took ten months to get him into the school. Having asked us to look at resources for Mark, the social worker and psychologist then decided that he should go to the Region's resource, even though it was unsuitable for him. It took three Children's Panels (the panel members were the only ones on our side) to get Mark to the school in Fife; it was only then that the social work department discovered they could not apply to send Mark there as it was not on the social work department list. So we had to start all over again and have Mark assessed by the Education Department. Confused? So were we, as we thought the funding was to be jointly shared by the education and social work departments. Eventually the papers went to the school and I had had several conversations with the headmaster over the previous months. Once the papers were received he telephoned me and said that his staff had looked at Mark's papers and decided that he was very suitable for the school, but they were very unsure that *we* were suitable! It is left to everyone's imagination as to what these papers contain – we were not allowed sight of them. We had obviously been labelled as interfering parents.

It is very emotionally draining to battle against such big institutions. As parents we had started believing a professional was just that, an expert, but very quickly discovered that this is not the case. They match the resource available to the child, but this may not be the resource that most meets his/her needs. We had started out being quiet and accepting, but very soon learned that you have to fight for every-thing a child needs. So much for the child being the most important part of the system – it is, in fact, the system that is more important than the child – this is how it has seemed to be for us.

Mark progressed well at the new school initially, but as the time came to leave and the uncertainly of the future loomed ahead he slipped back. It was an excellent school and my only criticism of it was that there was no preparation for the child to enter the outside world of work at sixteen. As with most older adopted children, he was immature in some ways for his age and there was no progression planned for the next stage in his life.

Mark is now a salesman and is sorting his life out.

Andy

When Andy came to us he had just had his fifth birthday. His entry into primary school had been delayed by one year due to his immaturity. I got him into nursery for two half days a week. Andy had difficulty relating to his peers and he was desperate for friends – his behaviour was often inappropriate with classmates and he tried to buy their friendship. He was a poorly co-ordinated child, he walked like a three-year-old, could not use or hold a pencil, could not count above three, and had limited language. He was very desperate to have a family of his own and we were Mummy and Daddy from the first seconds of his meeting us. You could tell that if he woke up with puffy eyes and a scowl, you were in for a bad day. Later we found out he was allergic to yellow food colouring, E102 (tartrazine), as well as other things. This resulted in him becoming a raging bull within ten minutes of him eating E102. Even though he had problems, I found him on the whole easy to deal with as he was an open and talkative child.

When Andy started school he was lucky enough to get an excellent teacher, whom he had for three years. In his first year he used to hit and scratch other children. When he had had enough and could not cope he used to sit under his desk with his cardigan zipped up over his head and throw his shoes across the room. I found I had to remove him from school for a week each term as when he became more tired, his behaviour deteriorated. I did this for several years until he could cope. This always resolved the problem by taking the pressure off him. His teacher was amazed that he managed to learn at all in Primary 1. She felt if he had conformed to normal social rules then he would have done well. At this stage, I was up every day in the classroom. By Primary 2 I was up weekly, and by Primary 3 I was up once a term for problems. Andy was still not an easy child but was progressing well. He attended remedial tuition in Primary 3. The remedial teacher was surprised when his class teacher asked what work she was doing with him – apparently no other teacher had ever asked! I had thought there was an integrated approach to teaching, so as to benefit the child to the maximum. At the end of Primary 3 Andy was assessed by the psychologist. We discovered he was dyslexic. At this stage, we were worried by his move to the upper primary and a new teacher. However, our fears were unfounded. He progressed well and we were only called up once in that year, and that was in the third term. By the next year we would not be up at all if the pattern progressed!

Andy had a new class teacher in Primary 5. His psychological report had said he should have as few changes as possible, but the school moved him to another teacher, even though his own teacher was moving on to a Primary 5 class. Within three weeks we were up at the school. I knew this year was not going to be easy, and soon I was worried. Andy had been a child who built intricate model cars of lego, but was now only building his sister's Duplo in a stack and knocking it over. He stopped swimming and skiing and would not tackle anything new. He was also becoming depressed.

I asked to see his teacher, as there were no parents' evenings that year. I was horrified. She had withdrawn the small things he did between tasks. For a dyslexic child, the effort required to do any piece of work tires the child more than usual. Letting Andy paint for ten minutes or play with cars helped him to recover and move on. She had stopped the painting as he was knocking over the water, and reasoned that he therefore did not deserve to play with cars. She complained that after the maths lessons, which he obviously understood and answered well, he went away and wrote a lot of rubbish down. When I explained that he was dyslexic she went into a flap saying she knew nothing about dyslexia and would have to see the headmaster!

There were many other things that we felt were not right. I rang the psychologist who suggested I wrote it all down, and that he would arrange a meeting at the school. I have no training in education but had a friend who was a specialist in special education. I found her invaluable. No one tells you what your child is entitled to or how to go about finding out, but she was very helpful and explained what we should ask for. We attended a meeting and I presented my observations and possible solutions to Andy's problems. This had the effect of the teacher being unable to teach for three days after it! The headmaster told me she was the best teacher in the school and the only one who gave him a forward plan for her class every week. It was obvious Andy did not fit into her neat plan and she could not cope with him.

Suggestions were made that special education should be considered. Time went on, and a month before Easter we had a very depressed child on our hands. The headmaster had an interview with my husband John. He had no solutions for Andy, except his exclusion. John suggested that he wrote to the Education Department, requesting a classroom auxiliary for Andy until he moved school. (This suggestion had been ruled out by the headmaster in the previous November as there was no money available.) We then withdrew Andy from school. John decided to contact the Education Department himself. After being given the run around initially, John threatened the department with the possibility of media exposure and legal intervention from a lawyer specialising in child care. Within the week we were offered a teacher for Andy for the three weeks up to the Easter, mornings only. After Easter we were informed that the department had found the money, a term earlier than they had expected, to employ another teacher at the special unit in a nearby town. Andy would be joined by five others in the class. Needless to say no one else joined him for a term. The headmaster said he would put Andy back in school in the afternoons (with the teacher he had failed with) until the transfer occurred. We had suggested that Andy went back to his last year's teacher who had an equivalent class, and with whom he had succeeded. However, we were told this was not possible as the child would be seen to be manipulating the system! It struck me once again: who was interested in the child's needs?

The new unit was superb. The headmistress and her staff were excellent. Andy progressed well, though not without incidents. It is a shame that children like Andy have to be educated away from their own neighbourhoods. They already have problems making and keeping friends, and the travel made a long school day. The headmaster in Andy's first school thought there were about five or six pupils in each year like Andy who needed extra help. He explained he would not consider asking for help as he would be seen to be unable to run his school. It seems that it was easier for the school to let the children go under, or move them somewhere else, rather than to fight for them.

With the psychologist's help we looked at secondary schools. We chose a small academy with a special unit which had an excellent headmaster. We found all the teachers helpful and interested in the children and their needs and how to meet them. The school was managing some of the most difficult children in the system. Some were in mainstream education and succeeding, despite having been out of education for up to nine months due to failure elsewhere. What a difference good leadership at the top of a school makes! Andy spent half the time in mainstream classes in the school with unit support, and the other half in the special unit.

There were difficult times for Andy but he did well. Unfortunately the term before he was due to leave, the school was closed. It was only a few weeks before the closure that the children were told where they were to move to. It was a testing time as change worried them and they needed to know where they stood. The closure upset Andy. Still, he went on to a college course, but was unfortunately unsupported by any special facilities, and he found aspects of it difficult. It is unrealistic to put these children straight from special education into the "real world" without support.

After much upset, Andy is now succeeding in life as a double glazing salesman.

Zoe

Zoe, our youngest, came to us at fifteen months. She has been much easier to raise as normal discipline rules work with her. She went to playgroup at three and education nursery when she was four years old. She was a timid child who did not like new situations, did not mix well in a group, and tended to look on as others played. She went to school just before her fifth birthday. Even though she had seen her teacher every school day for the previous two years, she did not speak in class, found pencil work hard, and at the end of Primary 1 could not read a word. I asked for her to be assessed in Primary 2. The result revealed that she had an auditory perceptive delay. This meant she had difficulty in interpreting sounds – she could not, for example, hear that ring and sing sounded alike. The teacher thought she was deaf, in spite of this not being the case. By the end of Primary 2 she was still not reading a word. We went to see the infant Mistress with a list of how the school had not met Zoe's needs – she had a similar list and agreed with us.

In Primary 3, Zoe was taught by old-fashioned methods which *did* meet her needs and she started to read. No one could test her spelling ability as it was so poor that she did not register on a scale. In Primary 4 she had a super teacher for half a term who then left and a supply teacher was appointed. We muddled through. Primary 5 was a good year. At that time we had problems with Mark and his secondary school and as a family we decided that we could not stand it if we had another child at this secondary school written off the way Mark had been.

Zoe was not a bright child and was in the lower groups academically. We decided to move her to the private sector and found a small prep school nearby, which accepted her. She hardly spoke for the first three months in class and did not mix with her peers. The school received the psychological report we had commissioned; it said her functioning IQ was 80 written and 84 verbal, and that she had an auditory and visual memory problem. I had always thought of her as just below average intelligence. The school must have wondered what they had taken on! Luckily they felt she had a higher IQ than the one she was displaying.

As Zoe had not been able to read until well in Primary 3 she found maths difficult to do as so much of it today contains language. In the local state system she did not receive remedial maths as they only offered language training. She was only attending PE and music classes once a week for one term a year. At nine, Zoe could not catch a ball. By eleven she was playing in a netball and rounders team, and though not their best player, she acquitted herself well. She played games every day. She now plays the recorder, is in the choir, and has started piano lessons. She loves music in general. The last assessment of her IQ showed, after two and a half years, that she was performing at 91 and rising. She is moving on to secondary school soon, going back one year to S1 as she is still emotionally immature. We have chosen another small private school as we could not find a suitable school in the state system. She will never be academic but hopefully she will reach her potential and be a happy fulfilled adult.

Conclusion

The educational problems we have experienced have taught us that you have to be single-minded in your pursuit of what you think is right for your child. You will sometimes be unpopular, but no one else is going to fight for him or her. I was sick of hearing 'but we have another twenty four in the class'. We learned to ask around to find out what is available, use local support groups for suggestions, ideas or for people to contact who have had similar problems. When extreme difficulties arise then a family will need support, as it can be very upsetting and affect all family members. An educational psychologist said to us, 'This is what your child needs but I cannot get it for him'. He advised us that pressurising the system we would probably be able to get an appropriate resource! I have to say it works. It takes a lot out of you both individually and as a couple. You have to learn to communicate well with each other or you will go under. It is a shame that whatever a child needs has to be fought for, and one wonders what happens to the children whose parents are not as persistent and articulate. I realise our problems may seem extreme, but I am sure many people can identify with some of them.

I am active in the Lothian Adopters Group (LAG) and have dealt with many families who have problems. This has led me to believe that older children being placed for adoption should have a full psycho-logical assessment done prior to the placement. This has two functions – firstly, to assess a child's educational, social and emotional abilities and so identify problems which can then be dealt with and secondly, to use this as a yardstick if difficulties arise later. This should be done by an independent person, as we have learned that people in the system only recommend what they know they can resource, not necessarily what the child needs.

It is a cheap option for local authorities to place children for adoption without active post-adoption support and it is naïve of us to think we can manage without it. It is important for adoptive parents to understand from the beginning that it is no failure on their part to ask for help. The children being placed are some of the most damaged in society and it is unrealistic to think all will be well once they are placed with us. As adoptive parents we are prepared and "chosen" because we can cope. It is important we ask for help whether it be with educational matters, behavioural or any other problems, before a crisis point occurs. We are not superhuman. We do not train ordinary people as parents in this country, so what chance have we with the most difficult of children. We have a telephone helpline for LAG members and often someone will say to us that everything is fine, and then be on the phone for over half an hour. Sometimes it only needs another person to talk to, to share the difficulty. At other times more professional help is required. The educational years can be difficult and stressful but all the effort is worth it for the child in the end. It is also important to bear in mind that every stage passes even though it may seem like an eternity at the time.

5   The use of residential schooling in sustaining adoption placements

Beth Gibb

Beth Gibb is an adoptive parent and Co-ordinator, Parent to Parent Information on Adoption Services (PPIAS), Strathclyde.

Our adopted children, Steven and Jill, came to live with us when they were seven and five years old respectively. As natural brother and sister, they had spent the previous four years together in a local authority children's home, where their parents had visited no more than twice a year. On the last visit, their mother introduced Steven and Jill to her new partner and their ten-month-old son. I do not know if that last meeting of the original family was considered to be a farewell meeting or not.

We were introduced to Steven and Jill about six weeks later. As we lived very close to the children's home, the introductory period was fairly intense, with the children coming to our home after school, two or three times a week at first, increasing to four or five times a week with an overnight stay some several weeks later. The children moved into our home on a fostering basis three months after that. However, I do not believe that the children were adequately prepared for the move at all. There were no life story books and we did not receive much information about their birth family and their early years. They had not been told that we were to be their permanent family – they thought they were coming to us for a holiday – and we attempted to do a lot of this work after they had moved in.

Both children were extremely active and did not like sitting still, except to watch television when they appeared to be totally absorbed. At the beginning, we had difficulty encouraging Steven to give up his role as "head of the family", but neither of the children showed a lot of reaction when we took over the parenting, except that Steven now tells me that he did not trust us or any other adult to take care of him, and he thinks that Jill only trusted him. He has not elaborated or explained this remark, so I have taken it at face value.

As the children's home was very close to our home, it was not necessary for the children to change schools at the same time of moving into our family. Steven and Jill were aware of the change of status that the move into our home brought. They had learned that to be living in a children's home was not normal, as they had both started to make friends with children who were living with their mothers and fathers in families in the neighbourhood.

After one year, because the classes increased in size and many of the classes were "composite" with only one teacher for over thirty children, we moved both Steven and Jill to two separate primary schools, which had smaller classes, more discipline, and more activities. School reports had commonly read 'Could try harder', or 'Shows interest in this subject, but does not always concentrate', or 'is too busy minding other people's business and interfering with other children's work'. With smaller classes and more individual attention, both children made reasonable progress.

We were aware, very soon after meeting Steven and Jill, that their co-ordination was poor. Neither child could catch a ball when it was thrown to them. Their letter and number formation was not as developed as that of their contemporaries, and their "colouring in" skills were very poor. Jill could not count to twenty, although she had attended school for one year. Through a teacher and a parent at Jill's school, we were introduced to a centre for neurophysiological psychology which specialised in educational difficulties. The director of the centre diagnosed both Steven and Jill as having minimal brain dysfunction and mixed laterality, which means they had a mixture of right and left dominance, such as having a dominant right eye, but a dominant left hand and foot. The exercises that were recommended took each child half an hour every day. They had to be supervised and we found that evening time was best. One exercise consisted of cross pattern creeping and crawling with hand and knee touching the floor at the same point in time, and with the eyes looking at the fingers of each hand as it moved forward. Another exercise was for the child to follow the beam of a small torch held first to one side of their head, and then repeated on the other side, as it described circles and figures of eight in the air. A third exercise required the children to splay and close the fingers in one or both hands in a rhythmic fashion and to lift the arm from the shoulder, turning the head to look at the fingers. Having persevered with exercises for over two years, both children became excellent swimmers and skiers, and Steven played in the school rugby team. Being able to take part in games and sport was helpful in socialising with their peer groups, where they felt able to function at the same level. This had obvious effects in raising the children's self-esteem.

Jill

Jill, who was sustained at primary school, had a lot of problems at secondary school. She was unable to cope with moving from classroom to class-room, often getting lost and arriving late for the lesson. She liked to act as "the class idiot", because of the attention it brought. She was disrespectful to the teachers and irresponsible in taking care of her books and pencils and turning in homework. She would swear and blaspheme and did not care who heard. She also distracted the other pupils from learning. The school persevered until she was thirteen years old, although she was suspended on more than one occasion and we received a letter stating the difficulties of keeping her in school. We tried two other secondary schools, where she lasted two terms and one term respectively, with many suspensions. After this, we realised that she could not cope in secondary school and that we needed some help.

Although there were difficulties at school, her behaviour at home had been manageable, until the final dismissal and the start of a long period of being at home, which was only broken by some tutoring in English and Maths and visits to an adolescent section of a local child guidance clinic. During this period when Jill did not attend school, I became aware that our control was slipping and her behaviour outside the home began to give us concern. On one occasion she was taken to the police station in a police car, which had been summoned by an army colonel on whose property she had trespassed and at whom she had sworn. This resulted in her being "locked up" for one night and being taken to court the next morning.

Having asked for the involvement of an educational psychologist, control of the situation began to slide from our hands. I found this difficult, as although I trusted the psychologist to make suitable suggestions to us, I was also aware that there was nothing available that was tailor-made for Jill's needs. This would have been a school within daily travelling distance of home, where the classes were very small, 6–8 per class, and where teachers were sympathetic and had insight into her emotional needs.

After eight months, a place was found at a list "G" school. This was a residential school, which specialised in children who had emotional difficulties and was paid for by our local education authority. There was absolutely no choice in determining which school it would be and there was a gap of nine months between leaving mainstream education and starting in "special education". The classes were very small, only 10–12 pupils per class, but a lot of the children were so disturbed that there was not much emphasis on "learning". I felt uncomfortable handing over responsibility to a school which, when I visited, made me feel unwelcome and where there was no-one to whom I felt I could talk.

My gut feeling was that my daughter should still have close contact with us, but the school was over sixty miles away and did not encourage any regular visiting by parents. We wrote regularly and occasionally phoned, but rarely did we receive letters or have our phone calls returned, although my daughter came home alternate weekends and all holidays. I felt this school was a "containing" establishment until she reached school-leaving age and I would have been happier if there had been more emphasis on her education. Furthermore, I felt we had been deprived of two years of living together as a family. As Jill had already lived for five and a half of her first six years either in hospital or a children's home, I thought that she had not had enough time to become fully attached to her new family, having lived with us for only eight years. I felt her expectations of being rejected again were being fulfilled and she would have benefited from living at home with appropriate support being offered to the family.

At residential school, Jill met a residential worker whom she got along well with and in whom she confided. After two years, both Jill and the worker left the school but remained in contact with each other for several years. I felt this was helpful to Jill.

Jill left this school when she was sixteen years old. She started on a Youth Training Scheme in a horse riding establishment, but was asked to leave after six months because of inappropriate behaviour to clients and staff. She tried a second Employment Training Scheme, also in a riding establishment, but it closed down. After this, she found employment at a boarding kennels for dogs and cats and worked there consistently for three years, until she resigned on account of poor health. She then worked for six months at a petrol station. She is currently unemployed.

In retrospect, the two year "breathing space" of not being a "full-time" parent helped us to return to a less traumatic lifestyle. Although we had been determined to give ourselves respite and had succeeded for several years, it became more difficult in adolescence when control issues became major battles. When the children were home, I did not feel relaxed and found myself worrying about what trouble might be brewing. Only being an active parent every second weekend allowed us to relax and feel less stressed.

Steven

In primary school, Steven was often described as a "will o' the wisp", with poor concentration even in the subjects in which teachers felt he was able to do well. His behaviour in the playground was described as rough and sometimes aggressive. He often got involved in arguments and fights that did not concern him. He felt he could only be guided or instructed if the correct authority (according to Steven) was in charge. Some teachers found him no problem at all, but others found him difficult to control. A great deal depended on what particular mood Steven was in.

When he was between twelve and thirteen years of age, his behaviour became destructive and delinquent and occasionally his temper tantrums escalated beyond our control. On one of these occasions, he smashed the windscreens of both our cars and showed no remorse. We sought help from the adolescent section of the same child guidance clinic we had attended with Jill. I felt this particular behaviour warranted a psychiatric assessment. The psychiatrist recommended that Steven take a course of Tegretol (a calming down drug) to try to help him control his temper. Steven took this regularly for three to four years, although he often claimed he did not need it in the school holidays. This was the time we felt he needed it most of all. Control battles between Steven and myself were an everyday occurrence, usually about coming for meals or watching television. It was impossible to make him take his medication if he did not feel like taking it, and I suspect that is why so many situations got out of hand. It was only later that it was realised that my children could be described as suffering from an attachment disorder syndrome. I would have benefited greatly from training in parenting skills to help manage such youngsters.

Almost simultaneously the school authorities and ourselves felt that Steven should move from his current school. For us, it was a few incidents where we had to involve the police which led to our conclusion; for the school, it was Steven's involvement in fights which escalated out of control. We felt that Steven's needs could best be met in a private boarding school. We found a fee-paying boarding school about twelve miles away and after we explained the situation to the headmaster, a place was offered to him. We paid fees, but an "assisted places" scheme exists, so that entry is not confined to those who can afford to pay full fees. We chose this school because of its lack of sophistication, its small size and therefore small classes, and for its interest in sport.

The incident with the car windscreens brought us to the notice of the Children's Hearings Panel, the outcome of which was that Steven attend the designated school under a supervision order, although we had found this school ourselves. There was no educational psychologist involved as his behaviour at school was not giving as much concern as his behaviour at home. My understanding is that List "G" schools can only be used when there is an educational psychologist involved.

We were beginning to be aware that living at home was becoming stressful for Steven. Although he could have come home every weekend, he chose not to, and appeared much happier not to have much contact with us. This was hurtful, but I had begun to change my expectations, and was convinced it was the best arrangement for Steven. After the first few weeks, he settled down and enjoyed boarding school for the next four years. He was nearly nineteen when he finally left school with five standard grades. We attended all school functions, with or without Steven's approval. We wrote and telephoned regularly, although often he did not want to speak to us, and occasionally we would visit the school and he would choose actively not to see us, although we made sure he knew we were there. He excelled in rugby, skiing and swimming and went on several holidays organised by the school. He also enjoyed going on Scout and Scripture Union camps in the holidays, which again gave us a break away from parenting for short periods of time.

On leaving school, we organised events so that Steven did not return home to stay permanently. Holidays could still be fraught with difficulties. If Steven was in a bad mood, he could still become violent and manipulative. Through the helpful psychiatrist, whom we were still seeing, Steven moved smoothly from boarding school to living in a hostel connected to the catering trade. He had shown interest in catering during his last year at school, and we had made contact with a hotel manageress, who was interested in helping young people start on a career in catering. She was an ex-police woman with experience in dealing with young men and women in the transfer from school to work. She organised that Steven return our house keys to us and he then received a key to his room in the hostel.

Steven is now twenty five years old. He has moved out of the hostel and is living alone in a flat. He is responsible for his own bills and bank account and has made friends with some young people living near by. His employment record has not been particularly steady, holding down jobs for a maximum of six months at a time. His jobs have recently included being a bouncer at night clubs and a security guard for a security company.

The benefits of residential schooling

I feel there is no one type of schooling required for adopted children. As in all families, there are different reasons and feelings around children's education. However, residential schooling can help the family regroup and be in a position to change unhelpful dynamics within the family. The emotional needs of the children are the most critical needs of all. If post-adoption support can highlight this and have psychological services built in at the time of placement, then perhaps progress at school can be monitored regularly. Families can be helped to make the best decision for the children and the family, as in situations where the child has an educational "record of needs". It would be helpful if adopted children had a record of "emotional needs" which would assist teachers, parents and others working with them to understand them.

I was aware that we were one of the first families in our area to adopt older children and that there would not be a lot of experience available for us from which to benefit. Sadly, on the very few occasions we did contact social services for help, the timing, the knowledge and the appreciation of the situation were so poor, that we sought help elsewhere with better results. It was also very depressing to discuss the situation with professionals, who clearly did not see the situation the same way we did! I feel it is absolutely essential to get help only from people who appreciate the whole situation and with whom the family feels entirely comfortable. Originally, we expected the professionals to know more than we did, but frequently this was not the case.

A break away from parenting, especially where children are emotionally disturbed and are feeding off the adoptive parents' emotions, is a wise move in preventing breakdowns in the family. It boosted our morale to be able to get help and advice about schooling, when we felt it was needed, because by this time we were feeling pretty useless as parents. We were pleased to be involved with decisions regarding future plans in the children's education.

The benefits of residential schooling outweighed the drawbacks for our family. As parents, we were not coping well with the "acting out" behaviour and were aware that both children were beyond our control. Holidays spent at home usually started well with everyone keen to help and co-operate with simple chores and an enthusiasm to do their share of tasks. After four or five days, however, attitudes changed and old habits of unco-operation, swearing, lying and being physically aggressive returned. At school there were recognisable authorities in charge, who were not bound emotionally to the children. At Jill's school there were also "care staff" in the form of residential social workers. The drawbacks of residential schooling included the children being separated from their friends and acquaintances and not being able to sustain friendships with local children.

In the long term, residential schooling helped to preserve our newly formed family attachments to each other, which were in danger of being severed by the extreme "acting-out" behaviour of both children, that we, as parents, did not understand or know how to control. Both types of school encouraged physical activities and offered help outwith the boundaries of the classroom. One of the lessons we learnt was that it was in everyone's interest to "go public" and be honest about identifying and recognising difficulties. If anything, we may not have acted soon enough in Steven's case, as he was nearly fifteen years old when he moved to boarding school in the middle of the school year. It would have been better if he had started at the beginning of the previous year. We failed to grasp the significance of small incidents becoming more frequent and tending to escalate in severity. We could have made a change while we were still in control rather than waiting for a crisis.

Although residential schooling was extremely helpful and, in fact, a necessity for our family, it is not likely to be necessary for all adoptive families in the future. It may be possible to sustain children for longer periods in appropriate day school settings if both the families and the children have adequate preparation before coming together and where there is competent, relevant and well-timed post-adoption support available. This can help families deal with difficulties as they arise and help them plan for the future in areas such as schooling.

6   Coping with trauma

An adoptive parent who now works as a Residential Child Care Officer writes about her experience of coping with the long-term effects of early deprivation and abuse, and why the backing of a comprehensive post-adoption service is so essential.

For the protection of the identity of her two adopted sons the writer wishes to remain anonymous.

It began almost twenty years ago. We could not have children of our own so the alternative appeared simple – we would adopt a family. We made enquiries over a period of eighteen months before finding an adoption agency willing to accept our application. We agreed to consider adopting older children, as there was a long waiting list for babies and no guarantee that we would be successful.

Our assessment consisted of a social worker interviewing my husband and myself in our home on several occasions. It felt as if we were sitting a test where we had to provide the right answers to a series of questions. We were young, enthusiastic, and had no idea of the enormity of the task we would be taking on. The social worker vaguely mentioned that some children being placed for adoption had been physically abused. Nothing was said about sexual abuse or emotional damage and the long-term implications such early life experiences would have for any child placed with us. We received no training during this process to help prepare us.

Our oldest son was placed with us one year after we were approved as prospective adoptive parents. He was two and a half years old. We were given little information about his background, but were told he had moved several times between members of his birth family and foster carers. Six months after he was placed, at my insistence, I received a few more details about his past and discovered that coming to live with us was his fifteenth move. At the time I did not understand about the effects of separation and loss on young children or the resulting lack of trust in adults. We did our best to parent him and felt at first that the emotional and behavioural problems he displayed must be due to a lack of skill on our part.

Our son was a bright little boy determined to be in control and to endeavour to parent himself. He resisted our attempts to bond with him and his behaviour often seemed obnoxious as he screamed a great deal of the time if he did not get his own way. He constantly wet and soiled himself and toileting problems were to continue into his early teens. We got a dog and he gained comfort from our pet more than from us as parents. I remember the first time we took him on holiday, he became distraught when we started to pack suitcases. I now realise that he thought he was moving again. Events in our family life began to get easier for him when they were repeated for the third or fourth time. Completely new experiences such as going to school, which had no past memories for him, also seemed to help. He formed a degree of attachment to my husband first of all, but for a long time the nearest I had to any bonding was that I felt fiercely protective towards him.

Our youngest son was placed with us three years later at the age of four. He was still in nappies, ate with his fingers, stiffened to touch and was unable to smile or cry. There was no fight left in him, his spirit had been broken. Again, the information we received had been scant. We were told that his behavioural problems such as lighting fires and urinating in corners were due to poor parenting and neglect by an alcoholic birth mother. There was no suggestion that he had been abused. When he was sixteen we gained access to the shocking details contained in his adoption file which revealed that he had been seriously physically and sexually abused while living with his birth family, in between numerous short-term admissions into care. I eventually formed a meaningful attachment with him when he was thirteen because he underwent major surgery and as a result was completely dependent just after the operation. However, all the tender loving care we gave him during the years he spent with us was not enough by itself to help him. My youngest son should have received intensive therapeutic help throughout his childhood to assist him in coping with the torture and trauma of his early life.

After the Adoption Orders were granted we had no more contact with the children's social workers. We had two highly disturbed children who competed aggressively with each other for our constant attention. It felt as if we were trying to keep a series of pots from boiling over and had to learn a whole range of strategies to manage without any explanation as to what we were dealing with. The boys' abnormal behaviour alienated us from the support of our family, friends and the local community. We were left isolated and full of self recrimination.

We had one social worker (who had been our worker at the time of our second placement) who offered to look after the boys on a voluntary basis one evening a month to give us a break. This was much appreciated but we really needed a far more intensive respite provision. A worker who could have built up a long-term relationship with the boys in order to support us would have made a significant difference to the high level of stress we endured. Respite could then have included this worker taking the boys out in turn so that we could give one to one attention to them both, and staying in our house with them to let us go away overnight from time to time.

Once both boys were at primary school we received help from educational psychologists who gave us welcome advice especially about behaviour management. This sustained us through our oldest son undergoing a severe regression to babyhood at the age of six, and a crisis when our younger son burned down a local barn without showing a glimmer of remorse. Along with this came the beginnings of some understanding that we were not to blame for our children's difficulties. But there was also a realisation that our expectations would need to be very different from those of other parents. Modifying what we must regard as achievements for our sons has been a long and agonizing experience.

To give our boys credit they tried their best to conform and there was laughter and sunny days with extremely happy memories. These times were a constant source of comfort to us as we struggled increasingly during their teenage years. At times, our oldest son's self esteem hit rock bottom – he would refuse to wash, keep the most undesirable company, and return home the worse for drink. It was a relief when the disruption this caused at school was over and despite his immaturity he then managed to complete an apprenticeship. In his late teens he had great difficulty about leaving home and refused to adhere to any limits on his behaviour – he wanted us to throw him out and repeat the rejections of his early years. We were determined he would leave in a positive way and kept taking him back until he got there eventually. He has been deeply affected by the problems of our younger son and at times these were so acute that his needs were overshadowed.

As our younger son approached fourteen his behaviour deteriorated. He was obsessive, had extreme mood swings, was physically violent towards others and self harming. I also became aware that he had enormous problems with his sexuality, but it took a long time to make sense of what was happening and to have the courage to admit to myself that he was sexually abusing children in the community without being detected. I wrote to psychological services to request their reinvolvement but it took six months to get an appointment. After two interviews the female psychologist said that it would not be safe for her to work with him on her own. I was advised to attempt to paper over the cracks by encouraging him to work towards short-term goals as he was in danger of disintegrating as a person. He would not co-operate with further psychological or psychiatric intervention and we were on our own. It did not occur to us to approach the social work department for help – we were unaware that in our area a post-adoption support service had started up. The staff involved in this service did not know of our existence either. Better systems are required for the future to make sure that adopted families are linked up to support services.

Our youngest son did not feel safe and desperately wanted security. He was a danger to the safety of others. We ended up turning our home into secure accommodation and working a split shift between us to keep him under supervision twenty four hours a day. We lived with constant fears of murder, suicide and imminent catastrophe. Eventually we could contain the situation no longer and just before his sixteenth birthday we contacted our local social work office and, after much deliberation, agreed that our son could be received into care for a three week assessment. At this point, we were provided with a highly experienced post-adoption support worker. For the first time we felt valued as parents; she understood and helped us to make sense of what had happened to our children in their most formative years and to realise what we had managed to achieve. She obtained the services of a professional counsellor who helped me cope with the terrible feelings of grief associated with the way our youngest son left home and the uncertainties that lay ahead. She worked alongside us to fight for a suitable resource for our son. She enabled a referral to be made to a psychotherapist who stated that our son would respond to therapeutic help but that this could only take place safely in a secure setting. However, to achieve a secure setting it looked as though he would first have to be charged with a serious offence rather than this being provided as a preventative measure. He went through three totally inappropriate placements including an awful period in a remand centre before we obtained a secure provision with appropriate treatment. Sadly this provision involves a full day of travelling from our home as such resources are so scarce. Our post-adoption support worker continues to be involved with us as we try to pick up the pieces of our lives and to ensure that our youngest son has the best possible quality of life in very difficult circumstances.

Our oldest son is about to become a father and our youngest son is now settled in a long-term secure psychiatric hospital. We maintain regular contact with both of them and our parenting task is still ongoing. I wanted to share some of what we have been through to let people understand why families who take on the care of children similar to our own should only be expected to do so with the backing of a comprehensive post-adoption support service.

7 Attachment disordered children

Caroline Archer

Caroline Archer is an adoptive parent and the Co-ordinator of the Attachment Disorder Parents Network (ADPN) for PPIAS.

Sometimes as I counsel adoptive parents from the Attachment Disorder Parents Network (ADPN) it seems impossible to find either reasons, or the right words, to encourage these desperate parents to go on sustaining their difficult adoptive placements. I find myself wondering what right I have to imply that carrying on giving to children and young people who give so little back (except for heartache) could be the right thing to do.

Children with Attachment Disorder (AD) can make family life virtually unsustainable. Their internal working model of relationships,[1] formed in their earliest years, has been tragically distorted. In their safe, permanent family placements they may perceive only danger and insecurity. Where they are offered acceptance, love and commitment they may experience only lack of self worth, mistrust and rejection.

A central feature of the attachment disordered child's history is traumatic disturbance to the attachment process in the first two to three years of life. Lack of adequate early nurturing, moves in and out of the care system, early hospitalisation or chronic painful illness, neglect and abuse can all prevent an infant experiencing consistent security and comfort. In turn this can lead to a failure to develop trust, self awareness and self worth and consequently poor cognitive and conscience development.

Characteristic behaviours associated with attachment disorders include an avoidance of intimacy or inappropriate demands for intimacy, extreme oppositional-defiant or passive-aggressive behaviours, aggressive and violent behaviours – including self-destructive activities. There is an apparent lack of conscience or remorse, with stealing and "over the top" lying, abnormal eating and elimination patterns, an abnormal eye contact often including the "look that could kill" and a superficial veneer of charm with non-significant others, associated with an inability to form healthy, meaningful relationships with significant others.

As if that was not hard enough to live with, adoptive parents frequently find it extremely difficult to locate appropriate understanding and support from professionals in the child care and mental health fields. The recent Report from the Social Services Inspectorate by Beverley Hughes[2] recognises that 'current availability of post-placement support is limited', 'access to services is "hit and miss"' and 'innovation has been limited to small-scale projects'.

What parents need

Adoptive parents have often spent many years questioning their own abilities as parents, blaming themselves for the problems within their family, and remaining understandably silent about their difficulties before finally attempting to seek help. At this point, when they are often exhausted and very vulnerable, they may be met with disbelief or criticism. Certainly they are unlikely to be able to mobilise the internal or external resources they need in crisis when met by resistance and disapproval from "experts".

What parents living with such troubled children do need is to be listened to, believed, and empowered to make their own decisions for their own children in an informed way. They need to be able to recognise clearly the increasing difficulties they are likely to face, since AD children tend to grow into their problems, and not grow out of them, and yet to know they are no longer alone and that there are strategies which can help. This is not a quick and painless process; indeed it takes courage and time to reach the point of moving on from paralysed helplessness to empowered parenting.

One of the most important tasks for those of us trying to help sustain such difficult placements is to validate the pain which families are going through, resisting the urge to move the family on before they have let go of some of the stored up frustrations, desperation and anger of years. Once this catharsis has been allowed to take place, the parents can make a clearer assessment of their current situation and begin to plan for the future.

Strange as it may seem, it often comes as a great relief to families to acknowledge just how bad things are. A common survival tactic has been to deny or minimise the difficulties, to forget the broken windows, the bruised shins, the expletives, the victimisation, the stealing, the lying, the wrecked plans, just as soon as a better patch arrives. To hear that this is a painfully common experience which can be named, one which will not get better spontaneously, and one which many professionals do not have a clear understanding of, can spur families on to greater efforts.

We need to acknowledge that AD children have been acting out their distress for so long that current family functioning is often poor. However, in doing so we must also recognise the imported psychopathology[3] which the child has brought to the family and, equally importantly, the strengths within the family which have sustained the placement thus far. Adoptive parents do need to hear that they have been doing a difficult job under impossible circumstances and that they are, and can continue to be, capable and competent people.

Parenting strategies

Parents of AD children need access to specific parenting strategies which work with such children. They have already tried out, and have found lacking, the gamut of "usual" parenting techniques. These appear to be ineffective because the child does not care whether he or she pleases the parent, gets a reward, or misses out on an expected treat. Such children get their kicks from frustrating their parents and being oppositional, and from the anger and discord they so successfully generate. Only in that way, by creating those feelings in us, can the child let us know how distressed and bad she/he feels inside.

It is a very delicate task for those of us providing support to inspire and empower parents of AD children, rather than to patronise, criticise or belittle their efforts. Frequently, things have been so difficult for so long that parents find themselves caught in a dysfunctional cycle of interaction with their child. Many have learned, like the battered spouse, to walk on egg shells, to anticipate and meet the child's unreasonable demands, and to placate in order to survive; others have tried to "tune out" from their children to avoid the conflict and the pain. Frequently, the ongoing stresses have led to relationship difficulties between partners and to stress related health problems.

Again, we would recommend taking one step at a time. If a parent can take on one issue they feel they can challenge with their child in one week, and succeed in breaking the child's stranglehold on the family, they will gain in confidence and dynamism for further battles. We explain that parents must only take on a control issue if they believe that it is in their power to win, since a win for the parent is also a win for the child. However, if the child wins the control battle, she/he will persist in unhealthy interactions and reinforce the negative cycle of anti-social behaviour.

Humour plays a large part in our parenting strategies. The best humour comes out of desperation and it is often possible to find something to laugh about in the most desperate and bizarre situations. Humour makes us feel better about ourselves (laughter can raise our catecholamine levels) and can defuse even the most potentially explosive of situations. Offering to sharpen the carving knife your child is threatening you with may take guts but it is infinitely better than showing your fear and feeding your child's urge to victimise, intimidate and destroy. Better still, it usually gives you the upper hand and takes the wind out of the child's sails. Members of the ADPN have produced a handbook of powerful parenting strategies for parents of AD children, entitled *Parent Assertiveness using Consequences with Empathy (PACE)*, available from PPIAS.

Sources of support
Parents are often in desperate need of a controlled break from their AD child. Respite, which is available as of right, when or before it is needed, with trained respite carers who understand the AD child's tendency to manipulate and make her/his parents out to be abusive or withholding, can make an impossible situation tolerable. Residential schooling funded by the local authority, where parents are treated as part of the team and where children are encouraged to take responsibility for their actions, to deal with consequences and to get in touch with their emotions, can also help to sustain even the most difficult of adoptive placements.

For many adoptive parents, it is difficult to have to accept that they alone cannot provide the loving, supportive environment they believe their child needs. Sadly, the response of many professionals can compound their sense of "failure". It is often argued that the resource implications of providing respite or residential schooling would be too great in the current financial climate – leaving hard-pressed parents the task of stretching themselves further to buy in the resources they need to keep the child within their family. A second common argument is that since the child's problems appear to stem from difficulties with attachments, it would further compromise the child's tenuous hold on family relationships if he/she moves into respite care or a boarding school placement. However, for many families this is the last resort and without it the child would certainly experience further the perceived abandonment and rejection involved in going back into the care system. With the support of planned residential breaks the family is often enabled to continue to provide a place in the family, and in their hearts, for the child until she/he is more ready to leave home in a controlled manner.

Many adoptive parents of AD children find that being linked to a network of parents in similar situations, like the ADPN within PPIAS and the Lothian Adopters Group, can provide them with an ongoing lifeline. The difficulties in their families are often so extreme that no-one who has not been there themselves can truly understand. Within a parents' network, information and experience can be exchanged on an informal basis. Families can make informal "buddy" links and help each other out through specific crises. Where friends and family begin to lose patience and empathy, since what they hear may appear so bizarre, another adoptive parent can provide the ear and voice of sanity. Just knowing that you are not alone, or imagining what goes on behind closed doors, can make all the difference. Self-help networks and specialist agencies can also provide information which may not be accessible anywhere else. Parents can be sustained through the hardest times by understanding why their child is like she/he is. Getting rid of the blame which has so often disabled the whole family can only come from knowledge of the child's early history and of the behaviour patterns of AD children. Interestingly, even severely attachment disordered children can take on board the reality of their lives if they are helped to understand that they are not intrinsically bad, however bad they may feel or act.

Children with the emotional and behavioural problems typical of attachment disorders will also benefit from facing the realities of their actions and accepting their responsibilities, rather than blaming anyone or everyone else for their situation. Older children who are testing out the idea of leaving home, since they believe their adoptive parents are "the pits", need to hear that the grass will not be greener elsewhere. Birth parents are frequently the subject of extreme idealisation, part of the AD child's polarisation of concepts and lack of integration. Again, these youngsters need to hear, and experience for themselves, that life will not become easier if they opt for premature emancipation, or go in search of their roots.

Adopted children "thrown into" families often throw themselves out again in adolescence, since their original experience of attachment and separation was interrupted. Adoptive parents can take comfort and be sustained through turbulent and painful separations, given the knowledge that this is not due to any failure on their part. Indeed even where the stresses in the family have become so great that the child has been received back into the care system, adoptive parents need to hear that they are still the most valuable resource for their child. Parenting does not cease when a child moves on and agencies must recognise the adoptive family as an ongoing resource. If the child is ever to learn about continuity and commitment, the adoptive parents need every encouragement to work through their own grief and to be allowed to be the best advocates and family for that child. We find frequently that after the dust of disruption has settled the young person is able to begin to value her/his adoptive family and begin to relate to them again more positively. This behaviour makes sense in terms of the approach-avoidance conflict which underlies much of the attachment disordered child's dysfunction and every effort should be made to foster these positive moves.

Empowering families

Living with an acting out, or acting in, child with attachment difficulties can leave the sanest person feeling crazy. It could be said that it is a measure of the degree of intimacy which has been reached within the adoptive family that the child's emotional confusion, turmoil, pain and anger are so deeply absorbed by close family members. Adoptive parents can take comfort from this knowledge, alongside the recognition that what they are experiencing is not in their imaginations.

It is difficult to talk about sustaining difficult placements without discussing opportunities for therapeutic change. Severely attachment disordered children understandably have very strong defences. They have survived by standing alone, protecting themselves and trusting no-one. They are unlikely to change the habits of a lifetime in the consulting room or over a sandtray! Over time, experience has shown that thera-peutic techniques which do not depend on building a trusting relation-ship, or on verbal access to memories and feelings, can be more effective in reaching severely emotionally disturbed children. Parent or therapist holding techniques are widely used in the USA in this context. It must be recognised that children with AD can have such a destructive effect on family life that time is of the essence. Many parents cannot afford to "hang in there" for years whilst conventional strategies, which often offer confidentiality to the child at the expense of family relationships, gently move the child towards change. Neither can the child afford to wait, since her/his anti-social behaviours increase over time and hence her/his inter-actions in the world become more and more negative. A brief description of holding therapy is given at the end of this chapter.

An intensive therapeutic programme, which uses intrusive holding techniques alongside life story and identity work, can provide an effective, coherent package of treatment over a relatively brief period. Following this breakthrough work, more traditional methods of working with children and young people can be increasingly usefully employed. Parents themselves can be encouraged to use "holding time"[4] in their own homes as a powerful means of getting through to their emotionally disturbed children. The "crisis of intimacy"[5] afforded by physically hold-ing a child through resistance and rage or grief to resolution can bring greater closeness and trust between parent and child and enhance com-munication with even the most avoidant of youngsters.

There is much that is still to be learned about sustaining the very difficult adoptive placements that AD children may present. What we have learned so far has been from courageous parents daring to speak out and tell it like it is. We must all strive together to realise the concept of parents as partners (I am sure it is no coincidence that these two words are almost anagrams). Parents are indeed the experts on their own child: even the most difficult placements may be sustained through the acknowledgement and validation of that expertise by supportive agencies. By empowering the family makers we give the child and family the best chance of making difficult placements work.

Frequently, partners within the same family unit will experience the AD child quite differently. In most cases, the adoptive mother takes the brunt of the power struggles, manipulation, rage, opposition and inappropriate demands. Not only are mothers more likely to be at home with the child for longer periods than fathers, but the child also tends to project repressed feelings from her/his birth mother and previous mothering figures onto the present mother figure. Clearly, if parents can be made aware of this phenomenon they can cope with the child more easily and begin to work as a team. Since the child may well use deliberate splitting tactics, on the basis of divide and rule, it is vitally important that adoptive parents are helped to recognise this issue.

Holding therapy

Children with attachment disorders have problems with touch, closeness and intimacy. In addition, they are well defended from their feelings and are often not aware of their own physical or emotional needs. Whilst these may have been adaptive features in their past, they can inhibit the growth of healthy attachment relationships and self-awareness in the present. Their behaviour patterns can remain highly resistant to change and can pose enormous difficulties for adoptive parents and therapists alike.

Many traditional therapies depend on the formation of a therapeutic alliance between child and therapist, and the use of language as the major medium of communication, and on allowing the patient to dictate the pace and direction of the discourse. In contrast, therapies which are being shown to be effective with children with attachment disorders do not presume on their capacity to form trusting relationships, to be able to get in touch with their feelings cognitively, or to move towards emotional health spontaneously.

Many forms of safe holding therapy have evolved over the past decade, with a variety of names such as rage reduction therapy, attachment holding therapy, dynamic experiential attachment process, and intrusive therapy. These therapeutic interventions have a great deal in common with each other and much which separates them from other more orthodox therapies.

The rationale behind intrusive holding therapies is based upon a theoretical understanding of the effect of disruptions to the infant attachment and development cycles, and on the practical understanding that love alone will not be enough, and that time is not on our side. Therapeutic holding provides a safe, containing "holding environment" for the emotionally damaged child, within which repressed primal feelings of rage, grief, abandonment and loss may be expressed.

The holding position reconstructs the natural nurturing position adopted by the mother and infant, and can model healthy sensory interactions for traumatised and abused children. It can operate at a non-verbal level of communication and can facilitate the accessing of pre-verbal trauma memories. It can provide opportunities for state dependent memory recall, and the chance to rewrite the tragic script of the child's past.

Holding facilitates the formation of intimate bonds between parents and children through the shared expression of passionate emotion. The therapist pushes the child towards emotional health, forcing the pace and forcing the issues: the child's maladaptive defence strategies are not allowed to come between her/him and greater well-being. Parents take over the holding as the child moves into the resolution phase. The child often regresses and will allow the parent to provide the tender nurturing which he or she missed out on in infancy.

The intensive nature of many of the holding therapies is significant in itself. Not only does it allow the child to go on working towards change and not retreat into a defensive shell between the (usual) weekly, one hour appointment, it can also incorporate more traditional methods of working with adopted children. Life story and identity work can become real emotional experiences using psychodramatic techniques, whilst the child continues to sense the relative safety of the holding situation.

The child is not allowed to control the holding situation. The child contracts to work hard on her/his issues but is not led to expect total confidentiality, since the therapist recognises the AD child's ability to manipulate, to triangulate, and to avoid speaking the emotional and literal truth. The child may respond initially with rage, but is sympathetically encouraged to take a more realistic view of life, and to recognise the potential for victimisation as well as the experience of being victimised. At every point the child is treated with great respect and can gradually learn both to receive appropriate compliments for positive responses and the comfort of good, safe touch.

Good intrusive therapists embrace parents as the prime agents for therapeutic change. They offer creative parenting strategies and empower parents to take back healthy control and power within the family. They recognise the dilemma which adoptive parents face in trying to show their children love and reasonable limits and readily acknowledge the dysfunction which AD children import, and re-enact, in each substitute family.

Reputable attachment holding therapists also recognise the potential for abuse of the strategies which they employ, and choose only to use them where other less intrusive strategies have been shown to be ineffective, and where the dangers of doing nothing outweigh the potential dangers of confrontive interventions.

References

1. Bowlby J, *Attachment and Loss (Vols. 1–3)*, Hogarth Press, 1980.

2. Hughes B, *Post-Placement Services for Children and Families: Defining the need*, Social Services Inspectorate, Department of Health, 1995.

3. Delaney R J, *Fostering Changes*, W J C, 1991.

4. Welch M, *Holding Time*, Fire Side, Bantam Books, 1988.

5. Crawford S, *Holding Therapy Pack*, PPIAS, 1984.

8 Adopted adolescents and their families

Peter Yeo

Peter Yeo is currently working privately as an Individual Counsellor, Trainer and Family Therapist. In 1994 he was employed by BAAF in Scotland to co-ordinate their Post-Placement Support Project.

At a recent workshop for adoptive parents concerning adolescents and their issues, sponsored by BAAF's Scottish Centre, I was struck by the considerable number attending whose children were several years short of starting their teenage years. The general feeling expressed was one of high anxiety at the prospect of one's adopted child becoming adolescent and the need to prepare by beginning to worry early.

It might be assumed that these parents' concerns simply echoed a view of adolescence as a time of emotional turbulence and rebellion as propounded by Anna Freud,[1] rendered more sensitive by the circumstances of adoption. Some, indeed, shared this concern, of anticipating reckless and angry abandonment by their young children. Others, however, dreaded the unending need to provide support and enthusiasm to highly dependent youngsters who lacked the support of a peer group as a result of their ability to withdraw from or alienate others. Such a view of adolescence (as a process of gradual steps) involving the mastery of new social skills both within and without the family, within a specific period of time, is represented in the writings of John Coleman.[2]

These contrasting viewpoints of adolescence, perhaps best described as the "dramatic" and the "evolutionary", will at different times appear more relevant in thinking about a particular adolescent. In times of crisis, all parents are inclined to forget the good work they have contributed to their young person's upbringing, with a corresponding slump in parental self-esteem. This can be particularly true for adoptive parents.

Mr and Mrs F had talked angrily about the worry their daughter

(Jane, 14 years old) was causing them both through acts of delinquency in the community and stealing at home. She had been adopted after being fostered by the Fs at the age of four. Her birth mother had been an alcoholic and Jane possessed early memories and current fears of police and ambulance sirens. The Fs' demeanour changed dramatically as they talked with pride and affection of school reports of Jane's progress, in playing in the school orchestra, quoting the words, 'she is a delight to teach'.

Temporarily, at least, the Fs could find release from the feeling that they were 'no good as parents for Jane', as an outside authority confirmed good qualities in her. Yet it would be human for them to resent school seeing the good side of Jane, and to wonder how much of her musical ability was innate, and how much the product of the relatively secure environment they offered. Often, I think, adoptive parents of adolescents feel like Martha in the Gospel story, where the humdrum consistency of regular family routines is undervalued by both the adolescent searching for their own identity, and often unwittingly by social institutions trying to help them.

The adoption double bind

Mixed loyalties regarding achievements and failures as a product of nurture and nature are only one of a number of mutually contradictory messages or double binds faced by adolescents and their adoptive families. Society asks individuals who form an adoptive family to act as if they have become a biologically continuous family and treat them accordingly with the award of legal status. Yet struggles with conjoint awareness and denial of differing physical characteristics, eg. colour of hair, eyes, skin, etc, change of name (particularly surname for older children) and incomplete information regarding origins, produce massive confusion for young people.

Bill

Bill (15 years old) described himself as going into "a daydream" on meeting a new teacher with the same surname as his birth parents which he had retained until the time of his adoption at the age of seven. Individual counselling allowed him to reveal the despair he felt he could not share with his adoptive parents at being torn between two worlds. While his "secret" remained with him and his counsellor, family work allowed the adoptive family to reaffirm their bonds to each other in the special circumstances of their creation, with a subsequent reduction in tension.

Tom

Tom (14) of African-Caribbean descent grew up in a Scottish community with no Black role models or peers. He expressed his dilemma by sleeping in the garden shed, feeling both abandoning and abandoned by both sets of parents, and spending considerable periods of time gazing at himself in the mirror. Family breakdown leading to removal to a Children's Home allowed him to vocalise his sense of worthlessness, confirmed (for him) by the colour of his skin. Contact with a peer group or exposure to Black role models would have reduced his sense of alienation considerably.

Adolescent sexuality and adoptive families

Adolescence like birth, the menarche and old age, is a combination of an inevitable biological process allied to the specific values that a given culture attaches to that process. The development of secondary sexual characteristics, and the onset of menstruation and "wet dreams" remind young people and their parents of the power of sexuality, both welcomed and feared. At the current time with teenage births outwith marriage at an all time high and the emergence (and fear) of AIDS as an almost apocalyptic scourge, parental anxiety regarding teenage sexuality remains high.

In adoptive families the issues can be particularly explosive. Issues of infertility and related low self-esteem for the parents may reappear at this time, while adolescents may be alternately delighted or appalled at their new-found ability to imitate the fertility of their birth parents, and sometimes triumph over the infertility of their adoptive parents.

Pete

Pete (16) became highly abusive of both parents, particularly his mother. While resisting the attempts of his adoptive parents to control him by stating they could not tell him what to do as they were not his parents, he also at times screamed and shouted obscenities at his mother. As she perceptively remarked, 'It is like he is shouting at someone else'. Later contact, following Pete's move to an agency supporting young people who were homeless, led him to reveal fears that his birth mother must have been a prostitute. This, allied to his own sexual awakening, left him with powerful feelings of disgust, excitement and hatred towards women, particularly regarding the fear of being coerced to produce unwanted children, who would then be abandoned by both parents. Discussion of contraception with an experienced male worker allowed him to relieve, at least temporarily, the fear of inevitably following in his parents' footsteps.

Thinking of, rejecting, or longing for birth parents, are usually part of the adopted adolescent's make up at this time. Images of procreation, birth, attachment and being given away or deserted may be conscious and are often preoccupying but rarely talked about. Often adolescents express the issues through a wish to find and look after the missing parent or parents.

Mary

Mary (15) adopted by her aunt after her mother had left the family when she was four caused considerable alarm in her large extended family by becoming suddenly distressed and weeping. A family meeting at an adolescent psychiatric out-patient clinic revealed that the adoption was an acknowledged fact but the cause of Mary's distress seemed like a family secret. Following an individual session with Mary, agreed to by the family, she was able to reveal with my support, her worries about her mother. This freed other family members to share their anxieties and worries and mourn the loss of contact dating over some eight years.

Post-adoption support

Post-adoption services are a relatively new phenomenon fuelled by both the trend of the adoption of older and "special needs" children, and by an increasing awareness of the complexity of the task in a society where expectations are vastly different from those of forty years ago. Specifically there is a much greater appreciation of the rights of all three parties in the adoption triangle.

Professional agencies charged with the task of helping adoptive families have often simply reflected the wider social confusion, by minimising the importance of adoption, and viewing family problems with adopted children as being simply an expression of dysfunction as in biologically continuous families. Family therapy, as often practised in child and adolescent psychiatry settings, has been a notorious offender in this regard, as complaints via adoptive parents' organisations attest.

Conversely adoption agencies, with their expertise in this area, may produce problems due to an over-concentration on this issue either intentionally, or by their very involvement which recalls earlier feelings of assessment (and being judged) for the parents, and a sense of powerlessness and being given away for the adolescent.

Defining the problem

Sorting out where to intervene between looking at the past, both pre and post adoption, the present, and even the possibility of a future, after the crisis, is an essential tool in post-placement support to adoptive families struggling with adolescence.

Donna

Donna (17) who was adopted at birth and her parents presented such a dilemma. The initial crisis lay in Donna's refusal to continue looking for work, having obtained several posts but quickly given them up, and a wish instead to hang around with friends from the local housing scheme, in contrast to the middle class area in which her parents lived and the peer group that lived there.

What was striking was the depth of parental rage which left the interviewer feeling an adoption breakdown was imminent. More out of faith than good hope, I offered a further appointment. To my surprise they returned and tensions had eased a little, allowing all parties to compromise a bit. Family meetings focused primarily on

Donna and her parents reporting back on agreed tasks concerning a search for appropriate work or training. On learning that her mother, Mrs S, regretted Donna's wish for greater distance in adolescence, I offered them a separate appointment.

For the first time Mrs S was able to recount her deep sense of grief at the death of her own mother when she was 15, and how she had hoped that her relationship with Donna would somehow replace that. The intensity of her loss had only struck her when Donna reached the same age and began indicating her need to separate. Both parents could share in this grieving process and revise their expectations of Donna more realistically.

In this situation, I did little to explore adoption issues, but instead concentrated on agreed practical problem-solving around an immediate cause for concern while offering space to listen to what was troubling Donna's parents, particularly Mrs S. It is possible that a focus on adoption would have raised insecurities where there appeared to be none and might have avoided the real issue.

In retrospect, I think that my ability to offer another appointment, despite the awful beginning, allowed the S family some hope that they were not so bad, and that perhaps rage and grief and anxieties about an adopted teenager becoming more self sufficient could all find their appropriate places. The ability to continue attempting to help as a neutral person, despite the fury of some adopted adolescents and their families, cannot be under-estimated.

Different services

The interweaving of individual, peer group and family support for adoptive adolescents and their families is essential. Groups offer a chance to reduce isolation, share common experience and develop a peer group – of particular importance to adolescents who feel different and friendless. Where race issues are important, such a group will need to challenge institutional images which are denigratory to black and minority ethnic cultures.

Similarly parents may feel that a trouble shared is a trouble halved and the support of a pressure group in campaigning for a range of services, including better schooling and a more supportive environment, is invaluable. Yet at times for parents, like adolescents, the number of problems to worry about can be overwhelming and also leave no space for highly individual and personal concerns. Hence the importance of individual support and counselling which is sensitive to adoption issues, and prepared to explore them when asked for, but is not driven by them.

Family support and therapy which allows for the special vulnerabilities of all parties (intrinsic to the paradoxical nature of the adoption contract, as it exists, which I liken to either a foster family or very small children's home, but with the social and legal status of a biologically continuous family) can be particularly helpful in resolving issues of day-to-day living, and at suitable times in quietening family ghosts. It is particularly important that underlying insecurities can be minimised by prior or ongoing individual, sibling or couple work outwith family meetings where necessary.

In closing, it is important to remember that adolescence comes to an end with the passage of time, whether it has been a period of tranquillity, uproar or dull misery for adopted adolescents and their families. Within the longer term perspective of the family life cycle if contact can be maintained through this period and beyond, then the adoptive family has survived and emotional bonds of support are strengthened.

I am reminded at this point of Jim (23) telling his adoptive mother that she worried too much about him while keeping contact with her chair with his foot, and of the colleague at the Association of Family Therapy conference telling me with pride about her adoptive daughter and declaring that she was now an adoptive grandmother.

References

1. Freud A, *Ego and the Mechanisms of Defence*, Hogarth Press, 1966.

2. Coleman J, and Hendry L, *The Nature of Adolescence*, Routledge, 1990.

9 Counselling adopted adolescents

Noel Whyte

Noel Whyte is an adoption counsellor on behalf of Lothian Region Social Work Department, currently based at Scottish Adoption Association in Edinburgh.

Over the past eight years I have been working as an adoption counsellor on behalf of Lothian Social Work Department. During this time I have had the opportunity of hearing the views of many adopted people, both young and old, and finding out what the particular issues for them and their parents have been. One of the key tasks of adolescence is to establish a secure sense of identity and to develop a feeling of self worth. It is the time when young people begin to ask all sorts of questions about themselves and to measure themselves against those who are important to them. Many adopted individuals find it impossible to answer these questions because of the lack of knowledge about their background and family of origin. The need for accurate information about the past is therefore extremely important.

The need to know

The age at which a child has been adopted is often significant. A child adopted as a baby with no personal memories and very little information about his/her background will have basic questions about who he/she looks like and where his/her particular interests or talents might come from. He/she will inevitably ask the question, 'Why did she give me away?' and may feel very angry with his/her birth parent(s) because of this perceived rejection. The adoptive parents may know some details about the background, but this might only contribute to their fears and feed into their feelings of insecurity, often leading to an overprotective attitude towards the child.

Where the child has been placed as a toddler or older, possibly with a history of neglect or abuse, he/she will have memories of his/her birth family, but these may be confused or even deliberately suppressed. The adoptive parents will also be aware of what their child went through and this knowledge may make it very difficult for them to feel any sympathy towards the birth parents. The young person can become trapped in a position were he/she is unable to admit to his/her own negative feelings and certainly cannot share them with his/her parents and cannot allow them the opportunity to articulate their hostility.

This inability of families to talk about the issues which stem from the adoption is a common feature. The parents may believe that they have been very open with the child about being adopted, but often there is a reluctance to bring the subject up again, or at least only on a very superficial level. There is a tendency to assume that the child is not interested if he/she does not ask any questions, but all too often the child feels unable to do so because of the fear of upsetting the parents in some way. A high proportion of adopted people who request background information, possibly with the intention of trying to trace a birth parent, will explain that they always knew they were adopted, but they could never talk to their parents about the subject and did not think they could do so at this stage. Many who subsequently do share their need to know more about their origins with their parents are often surprised to find a very sympathetic and supportive reaction.

Without good communication between parents and adopted child the fears and fantasies which come to the fore in adolescence can become quite unmanageable. The normal teenage rejection of parental values and beliefs has an added edge for adoptive families where there is often a difference in social and cultural background. Alarm bells can suddenly ring for parents if their teenager's choice of friends or interests do not match with their expectations. The young person may begin to fantasise about how wonderful their birth parents might be, particularly if they feel they are not being allowed enough freedom. When tensions rise, and in the heat of an argument, things can be said on both sides which are not easily forgiven or forgotten. Sexuality is always an issue and will be tied up with the legacy of promiscuity often inherited by the child. Adoptive parents may find it difficult to separate their feelings (sometimes unresolved) about their own infertility from their anxieties and fears for their child.

For some adopted teenagers the urge to kick against the traces will be curbed by their feelings of insecurity. Is it safe to rebel against adoptive parents? Will I suffer a further rejection? Should I be loyal and grateful? Fourteen seems to be a key age for adolescents to begin to express an interest in their birth family. Alternatively they can feel very hostile towards them, which may be the only way they can cope with their fear of their past. At this stage their curiosity is very self-centred and is not usually generated by an interest in the birth parent as a real person but only as an extension of themselves. Adoptive parents should not feel threatened. Very rarely will their teenager be looking for replacement parents, but simply for answers to the inevitable question 'Who am I?' A positive and sympathetic response can often help the young person not only to fill in some of the missing pieces in their personal jigsaw, but also to strengthen relationships within the adoptive family.

Jenny

Jenny, aged 14, seemed obsessed by her birth family; in fact, she wanted to go back to live with them. This became such an issue that her adoptive parents approached the agency which arranged the adoption to ask for their advice. The agency suggested looking up the records and giving Jenny some non-identifying information in the hope that this might help her to sort out some of the confused feelings she clearly had about who she was and where she belonged. When the worker was sharing this information with Jenny and giving her details of the family's physical description, including the fact that her brothers and sisters all had freckles, she was quite amazed at Jenny's reaction. 'Freckles! Oh, I couldn't have anything to do with anyone who has freckles!' No doubt Jenny's interest in her birth family will be renewed at a later date, but, for the present, this seemingly insignificant detail has been enough to change her mind completely.

Tony

When the "need to know" begins to prevent the young person from getting on with his or her own life it is always difficult for adoptive parents to know how to help. Tony was placed for adoption at the age of four years. His birth parents had separated and his mother, who had learning difficulties, had never managed to care for him adequately. As a result he had suffered neglect and abuse. Tony was always aware that he had a younger brother, Scot, who had been in care with him at one point, but never knew what happened to him. He assumed that he had also been adopted. By the time Tony was in his late teens it was becoming more and more important for him to find out what happened to his 'wee brother'.

Tony's adoptive mother realised how much this meant to him and was determined to do what she could to help. It was she who first approached me for advice. From the records I learned Scot had not been adopted but had remained in foster care with ongoing contact with his birth mother. After further investigations I discovered that he had returned to his mother on a permanent basis when he was ten, and was currently living with her and her second husband, who had recently adopted him. The situation seemed stable now but this had not always been the case. There were queries about the birth mother's lifestyle and Scot had obviously had serious behaviour problems in his early teens.

It had taken several months to establish these facts, during which time Tony, who was quite an immature boy, went through a difficult period himself. The knowledge that Scot had remained with his birth mother created a real dilemma for him as Tony had never been interested in finding her and his feeling towards her were quite negative. He was adamant, however, that he wanted to make contact with Scot and after much discussion with Tony and his adoptive mother, who remained firmly committed to seeing Tony through this no matter what the outcome, we agreed that I should contact the birth family on Tony's behalf. As a result a meeting was arranged between Tony and his adoptive mother, and Scot and his birth mother and her husband.

The process has helped Tony put to rest many of his fears and fantasies as well as reassuring him that Scot is well and happy. Tony now expects to remain in touch, but he realises that he has his own life to lead and it is not with his birth family. It has also strengthened his relationship with his adoptive family, particularly with his mother, who feels they have become much closer after a period when Tony seemed to be drifting away. There are also signs that Tony is able to concentrate on his career again, as he has gone back to college to complete the course he did not finish last year.

Black children and identity needs

When race is an additional factor in the adoptive equation there is an increased risk of the young person experiencing difficulties around identity formation. The need for detailed information about birth parents is even greater in these cases, as is the need for the information to be shared with the child as early as possible. It is not uncommon to hear black or mixed race children or young people placed with white families describe how they grew up believing they were white, or at least having completely absorbed the attitudes and values of their white parents, only to find that they were seen by the world at large as black. Many are left feeling alienated from both cultures and this sometimes drives them to all sorts of lengths to fit in to one or the other. Black youngsters can become obsessed with straightening their hair or scrubbing their skin, sometimes even bleaching it to become lighter.

Ben

Ben remained in long-term foster care from birth until he was ten years old, because his white English mother and black Ghanaian father were unable to offer him a home, although they maintained contact. His foster carers never saw it as their responsibility to talk to Ben about the fact that he was a black child living in a white family. Ben went on to two failed adoption placements. He was never able to settle and ended up in institutional care as a teenager. He is still trying to work out who he is. Perhaps if he had been placed in a family where one of the parents had been black this might have helped him to accept the black part of his identity. Alternatively, if the adoptive parents had received more help to focus on this particular issue both prior to the placement and once Ben was part of the family, the outcome might have been different. Part of the problem in this case

77

seems to have been a lack of recognition that there was an issue, both by professionals and non-professionals. It also seems to me to be a situation where quite structured ongoing support should have been built in to the second placement and not left to the adoptive parents to ask for help on an ad hoc basis.

Mark

Sometimes the lack of accurate information can lead to even more confusion and pain. Mark was a mixed race child placed with a white family. His adoptive parents were unable to tell Mark very much about his racial origins other than that his mother was white and his father was black. There was an assumption that he had been of African descent and as Mark was growing up he quite liked this idea and became proud of his African heritage. He certainly regarded it as superior to being Pakistani or Indian as he knew these communities were regarded prejudicially in the (predominantly white) area where he lived. Later when he wanted to find out more specific information about his background, he discovered that his father was, in fact, Pakistani. This has had a devastating effect on Mark, leaving him confused and angry and unable to concentrate on finding employment, making appropriate relationships, or laying down any of the foundations which are necessary for a healthy adult life.

His adoptive parents have been supportive to him throughout, actively encouraging him to seek out the information he seemed to need, and helping him as best they can to cope with the emotional upheaval he has been going through. If more attention had been paid to ensuring that accurate background information was available, and that it had been passed on to the adoptive parents at the time of placement, this situation need not have arisen. These parents were able to talk with their child about his adoption and about his racial identity, but the details they had were limited and they did not realise that help might have been available from the placing agency. Nor were they in touch with any other families who had similar experiences of adoption and who might have been able to offer some relevant advice. Both Mark and his parents have benefitted from the counselling which has been available to them. His parents regret that they did not seek out this kind of support at an earlier stage.

Supporting adoptive families

The task for any parent of an adolescent is never easy. How much more difficult must it be, therefore, for the adoptive parent where there are all sorts of unknowns surrounding the child, and where there may not have been the opportunity to establish the kind of unquestioning, all-accepting relationship between parent and child which is sometimes necessary to weather the storms of adolescence.

Knowing this, adoption agencies must play a more active role in providing post-placement support for these families. A range of resources should be available including individual counselling and advice, regular workshops and seminars and ongoing group support. In many parts of the country support groups for adoptive parents have been developed and have been very successful in providing a forum for families to meet on an informal basis, share experiences and advice and, together, to focus on issues of particular interest. Inevitably the kind of help and support available through this channel is reactive rather than proactive as issues are identified only after they have become areas of concern. It is the job of the professionals to offer the kind of support which will adequately prepare and equip families to deal with potential difficulties before they are overwhelmed by them.

Workshops on a variety of subjects such as talking to your child about adoption, how to cope with the birth family, parenting a child who has been physically and/or sexually abused, and many more, should be part of a regular programme on offer. These might be provided by the placing agency or by an independent agency offering post-adoption support. It is, of course, crucial that during preparation families must be encouraged to use these facilities and not to regard the need for them as a failure, but rather as an integral part of being an adoptive family.

Agencies must also ensure that families have full and accurate information about their child's background and be encouraged to talk about this with him or her right from the beginning. Some adolescents will still need to have access to such information from a source outwith the family. Advice about how they could gain access to it should be available to them in the same way as information about abuse, bullying, etc, through school guidance systems and other community counselling services aimed at teenagers.

In my experience group support for adopted adolescents is not very effective. They are much too caught up with their own problems and feelings to share with others. They benefit much more from individual counselling with a sympathetic and objective adult who will listen to their fears and wishes in an atmosphere free from guilt or pressure. This, again, could be provided either by the placing agency or by an independent agency. The growing practice of more open adoption, including regular exchanges of information, is a further way of ensuring that the child's past is not a closed book, but can, if dealt with sensitively, be a very positive and enabling influence on the child as he or she matures.

There will never be a definitive package which offers the magic solution to all the many difficulties adoptive families will face, especially as their children battle their way through adolescence. With the knowledge we now have, however, about adoption and about the risks we run if we try to ignore the difference between natural parenting and parenting by adoption, there must be more commitment to ensuring that a range of effective post-adoption services is available to adoptive families.

10 A family based respite care scheme

Sue du Porto and Rena Phillips

Sue du Porto is a social worker with St. Andrew's Children's Society, Edinburgh.

Rena Phillips is Lecturer in Social Work, Department of Applied Social Science, Stirling University.

Introduction

For families adopting older children and children with special needs, respite care is potentially a very valuable post-adoption resource. Ideally this can take several forms: family and residential based services, adventure holidays, carers coming to the family home, and sitting services. The reality is that such services are very thin on the ground. In this chapter we focus on the only family based respite care scheme in Scotland, operated by a voluntary adoption agency, St. Andrew's Children's Society, which is specifically targeted at adoptive families and long-term foster carers.

A recent survey of family based respite services for children in Scotland identified 21 schemes, with a wide geographical spread and providing flexible support for families.[1] Yet only seven per cent of respite care is provided by such schemes. Family based respite care is available to only 575 children, with 459 on a waiting list, of whom 285 have waited for longer than nine months. For some schemes there are shortcomings in support to staff and respite carers, in training resources, and a lack of adequate finances. The evidence is that family based respite is overwhelmingly a "white" service, with minority ethnic communities scarcely represented either as respite carers or as service users. Most importantly, from the perspective of adoptive families, the main criteria for access to these schemes are learning and physical disabilities.

Practice experience and research evidence so far suggest that respite schemes neglect the needs of children who are emotionally disabled through abuse or other traumas, as is the experience of many adopted children. Adoption workers give up asking for respite places in schemes that cater for physically and mentally disabled children as waiting lists are long. Indeed it could be argued that respite services should be designed for specific groups, and be attuned to their needs, rather than mixing people with different needs.[2] The experience of Parents for Children, a leading voluntary agency in London placing older and very difficult children, is that sometimes the local authorities running the scheme simply want to avoid blocking a bed. In other cases, a child who has been sexually abused is seen as a threat to other children placed in the family by the authority. Parents for Children believe that if respite care is to be of value to adoptive families it has to be 'practical, affordable and available when needed. A waiting list or an emergency scramble for help is a poor substitute.'[3] It is therefore creating its own respite care service, with a team of six carers, and adopters entitled to a set number of respite hours per month. The problem they face is who should pay for this respite care. The dilemma is that voluntary agencies may find themselves as rivals with authorities who have a respite care scheme, and may refuse funds on the ground that they already provide respite care, although there may be long waiting lists for the service.

The survey of family based respite services in Scotland described above did not include the St. Andrew's Children's Society respite scheme due to a lack of knowledge of its existence, indicating the marginal position of adoptive families vis à vis respite resources. Further evidence for this comes in a study of family based short-term breaks for children in need.[4] The authors focus on schemes for children whose needs are in danger of not being met due to their family circumstances, i.e. poverty, unemployment, social isolation, broken family networks, and single parenthood. Several models of service provision are identified, including short-term breaks in support of long-term foster placements, but no mention is made of the needs of adoptive families.

Family based respite care at St. Andrew's Children's Society
Setting up the scheme
St. Andrew's Children's Society started as the Catholic Enquiry service

in the 1920s, acting on behalf of single pregnant women who sought advice on whether or not to place their child for adoption. Alongside the counselling work, the Society prepared suitable couples who were usually childless and wished to become a family by means of adoption. With the changing face of adoption over recent years the role of the Society has moved accordingly, and placing older children with adopters has become the norm rather than the exception.

Adopting older children presented the Society's adopters with additional and difficult challenges. There was an increasing concern within the agency at the relatively high level of placements disrupting nationally because families had reached breaking point. They could no longer sustain the behavioural problems, lack of attachment and disruptive nature of the children they had adopted. There was a desperate need for respite, a chance for families to have some space and to take stock, without the necessity of the child being taken into care.

This was borne out by the Society's association with a local support group, the Lothian Adopters Group (LAG). They were constantly expressing concern at the limited supportive services available to them, both in terms of choice and post-adoption support. As a result, the Society set up a pilot scheme during 1991, with the aim of providing regular breaks, usually in the form of weekends and additional days in the holidays, to adopters and long-term foster carers, in a family environment.

One couple who had been through the adoption training and assessment was recruited to the scheme. At the time, they had felt unable to commit themselves to the full time care of an older child, because of their lack of confidence in their abilities to deal with very difficult behaviour. As respite carers they were paid a fostering allowance and travelling expenses by Lothian Region Social Work Department. At that time there was no financial remuneration for the Society's support worker.

The first experience of respite care was encouraging and beneficial to the adoptive family and the respite carers. It was felt that the timing was right to establish the scheme on a surer footing. In order to look at the viability of a respite care scheme, a survey was conducted with LAG. The encouraging aspect of the survey was that all the respondents felt that such a scheme was needed. The most frequently stated circumstances in which families would use the service were for emergencies, weekend breaks, the illness of a parent, or in caring for teenagers. Many people felt that respite care would alleviate pressures, tensions and stress within a family, and that simply getting a break would calm a situation and allow parents to recover from mental and physical exhaustion.

At present there are six respite carers, four couples and two single people, who offer seven placements. The usual pattern of respite on offer to adoptive families is one weekend in four, and some additional days during the holidays. Lothian Region Social Work Department financially supports the seven respite care placements presently in operation. This includes a payment to St. Andrew's Children's Society for the social work support, in addition to providing a fostering and mileage allowance to the respite carers.

From the start of the scheme it was considered important to have a regular system of relief for families, which was more productive in the long term than providing families with a break as a preventative measure in a crisis. Research has shown that social workers are not in favour of the practice of emergency intervention or "the sticking plaster approach" where a response is made only after a major crisis has occurred. This often results in the demoralisation of the clients and workers alike. Illustrating the above is an example of a respite care referral which in retrospect was not an appropriate one.

Case

The child in question had learning difficulties, severe behavioural problems and a complicated relationship with her parent. Although a psychiatric referral had been made by the child's social worker, no support was forthcoming, and respite was used as the only option available at the time. The family was at crisis point, unable to make constructive use of the respite care, and the breaks never progressed beyond a couple of hours. Although it could be argued that the respite in this situation was helpful in allowing the social worker to make a fuller assessment of the family situation, it did not relieve any stress on the parent or child and possibly added to it, particularly as two different respite care families were tried.

It is difficult sometimes to assess whether the referral for respite is an appropriate one, as the respite care worker has to rely on the assessment and information given by the child's worker. This becomes more complicated if the child's worker has just taken over the case and has little knowledge of the family and also limited resources available, with no specialised support forthcoming for the family. In contrast, in another situation where respite care was part of the future plan for the child, it has continued for a number of years. During this time, the child has had to cope with changes both in foster placements and in school, which have caused him great distress. Respite care in this instance has given him some experience of having consistent, caring and committed adults in his life.

Preparing for placements

This is crucial to the success of respite and involves certain key stages. Following the initial enquiry from the child's social worker, a referral form is completed which gives the respite worker some basic information on the child and reason for referral. At this stage a potential carer is identified according to availability, preferences and skills. Information on the respite carer is shared with the child's social worker and parents. A meeting is then arranged, not including the parents and child, where social workers and respite carers have the opportunity to address relevant issues such as assessing whether there is the possibility of a successful match.

The next stage involves the matching panel, which is either part of the Society's adoption panel, or a smaller panel convened at short notice. The matching meeting can be useful in terms of the consultative process for the respite worker. In addition to being held accountable, it also gives professional credence to the respite care service. A possible disadvantage is that it can slow down the matching process with yet another meeting to arrange.

Following the panel's approval the crucial visit can be arranged between the two sets of carers, where information is shared and people find out if they are comfortable enough with each other to proceed with respite. Vital in the whole process is the child's feeling towards the respite carers and the amount of preparation the child has had prior to the first visit. In some cases children were confused about the reasons for the respite arrangements. It is important for the child to be included in the family discussions with a social worker as to these reasons. The child needs ongoing support of a social worker, particularly to look at issues like being scapegoated and alienated from the family. Some families tend to single out the child as the problem, and use respite as a punishment.

If respite is an option introductory visits are arranged. The first one usually involves a visit to the respite carer's home by the parents and child. In the experience of the Society, most parents prefer a number of visits before any actual overnight stay takes place. This is preceded by a planning meeting where a contract is drawn up and various papers are signed, eg. parental agreement and medical consent. The introductory process alone involves a lot of time and commitment on the part of the respite carers who often also attend other child care meetings for some of the children they have in placement. Reviews are usually held after the first three months, or sooner if problems occur, and continue every six months.

Recruitment, training and support of carers

The necessity of recruiting the right people, and providing a good standard of assessment, training and support is of paramount importance to successful short-term care. Recruiting respite carers has proved to be a time consuming activity. Experience in family finding projects suggests that it is fairly standard to have to encourage a large interest in order to get the right families for this particular form of care. The Society's recent publicity campaigns both on the television and in local newspapers confirmed that the initial response is very positive. Unfortunately the drop out rate is high, as many people are unaware of the kind of involvement that is required, particularly in terms of working with the parents of the children.

Although the group training and individual sessions used in an adoption assessment are in many ways applicable to respite carers, they have not been geared towards understanding the particular issues involved in part-time care. Some of the more important ones are the need for communications skills, the need to achieve a good working relationship with parents, differing parenting skills, and limited involvement in the child's life. A disadvantage of the adoption assessment format is the time factor, as it is essential to prepare and assess people reasonably quickly in order to respond to the need. Unlike in adoption, it has proved more difficult to use group work with respite carers, as their numbers are fairly low, and so we have had to adapt our assessment and training programme. Currently we are using an adapted fostering assessment which does not require the same comprehensive amount of information. The respite carers are expected to complete the assessment form themselves, which gives them the opportunity to put their experiences, views and feelings in their own words and thus hopefully be more involved in the process. Training for the respite care role in a group context is more viable post approval and is part of the respite care support group. This group, apart from offering mutual support, has ongoing training sessions on topics such as working with professionals and parents and safe caring. In addition, the newly approved respite carer is linked to an experienced one who has the immediate "hands on" experience, which a respite worker might not have.

From the LAG survey it emerged that adoptive parents agreed on the following essential qualities in respite carers: patience, sensitivity, a caring loving attitude, flexibility, a knowledge and understanding of children's needs, resilience and a sense of humour. Many people also felt that potential carers should understand why such a service is needed, and not be critical of adoptive parents for requesting this type of support. The importance for carers and parents to work closely together was frequently mentioned. A vital element in the training and support of respite carers is that they need to see working with parents as a crucial and integral part of their task, and that contact and cooperation between the two parties are essential for children's wellbeing. In looking at the question of support for respite carers, it is interesting to note that often the relationship between parents and carers becomes a mutually supportive one.

Respite care can throw up potential areas of conflict between respite carers and parents. The differences in parenting styles, and the lack of acknowledgment of the strength of each others' skills does lead to a certain amount of friction. Although the introductory visits are used to allow the respite carers to become familiar with the parents' lifestyle and some of the do's and don'ts in the child's home, it is not always easy for the respite carer to compromise. This is particularly difficult when, as mentioned earlier, children perceive respite as a form of punishment. Another dilemma for the respite carer is the difficulty in creating a balance between a positive working relationship with the parents, who often use the respite care as a support in coping with the day-to-day stress of looking after children, and the respite carer being regarded as a "semi-professional" who attends child care reviews, and so on.

Other tensions might arise when respite care strongly emphasises the need of parents rather than children. It might be argued that if parents get some support and relief by using respite, then children will benefit as a direct consequence. Adopted children need continuity and security. The danger is that respite can mean another family in a long series of families. A balance is needed between providing a positive experience for the child, as well a break for the parents. In one respite placement a young person of nearly 16 showed signs of rebellion when the time came for her weekend break. Every indication was that she was feeling grownup and did not need to go away, although her parents still desperately needed a break. This situation has been temporarily resolved by trying to involve the young person in the practical arrangement of the break, and to foster a more "adult to adult" relationship on a "befriending" basis, between the respite carer and the young person. Similarly, it is helpful to recognise that older children often resent having to go away from their own home and friends, and alternative resources in their own community might be more appropriate.

Whilst post-adoption support is increasingly recognised, the complex area of costing post-adoption services has not been assessed adequately in financial terms. Good short-term care takes time, effort and money. Currently St. Andrew's respite care scheme is in part funded by Lothian Region SWD and a charity grant. In order to be self financing, the respite care scheme needs to expand and offering the scheme to other local authorities is being explored at present. This has proved quite difficult, which suggests that respite care for adoptive families is not seen as a priority by financially overburdened authorities. Having a greater pool of respite carers can potentially allow adoptive families greater choice of respite placement, and more flexible arrangements such as day or part day respite. The possibility of opening up the Society's respite scheme for children with physical and learning disabilities has been raised, but this would negate the advantages of a respite scheme designed specifically for the needs of adoptive families. The inescapable fact is that if respite care is to be available as part of a post-placement plan for adopted children, there is a need for secure long-term funding by local authorities to schemes providing such a service.

A user's view of respite care
The Brown family

'Adoptive families do not have enough information about respite care. I don't know how I would have got on without such help.' These are the words of Mrs. Brown who agreed to be interviewed about her views and feelings as a user of the St. Andrew's respite care scheme. She and her husband adopted Steven (12) and Ken (10), natural brothers, three years ago. They were previously fostered by the family for four years. Mrs. Brown had been a foster carer for twenty years, and had looked after 83 foster children in that time.

Between them, Steven and Ken have a long history of very troubled behaviour, including hyperactivity, destructiveness, and soiling and wetting. Mrs. Brown explained that decorating the house is difficult as the boys tear the wallpaper off and write on the walls. Steven is often up during the night and, for example, can leave taps running. He goes to special school and is due to transfer to secondary education, but two secondary schools "will not have him". Ken is beginning to have problems at school as well. Because of the boys' hyperactivity Mrs. Brown has always needed to be "on the go" in order to keep them occupied. Safe and attractive playing space in the neighbourhood is limited, and she takes them for walks in the evenings. She has become involved in local play schemes during the summer so that the boys can take part. Because of the amount of attention the boys require, Mrs. Brown has given up her job in a local playgroup, and money is very tight. Despite a catalogue of difficulties, Mrs. Brown has a strong commitment to the boys and the quality of their lives.

Respite to the family was started when Steven and Ken were fostered, and it was agreed that respite was essential if the adoption of the boys went through. There was only one family to choose from, Mr. and Mrs. Smith, through St. Andrew's respite care scheme. After introductory visits and an overnight stay the boys went to the Smiths, one weekend in six, for a period of about four years. The Smiths would pick up the boys on a Friday afternoon and bring them back on a Sunday evening. This arrangement has recently come to an end as the Smiths are in the process of adopting a young girl they have been fostering. They feel that she is increasingly finding it difficult to cope with Steven and Ken's behaviour, particularly their language and sexual innuendos. The respite arrangements will continue with Mrs. Brown's daughter and a friend of Mrs. Brown, who both live locally, sharing the care of the boys one weekend in four. The friend has been assessed as a carer, and the social work department continues to pay respite fees to both parties. A possible respite care family was identified in the scheme, but they felt unable to handle Steven and Ken's difficulties.

Mrs. Brown feels that she was fully consulted and involved in the respite care arrangements, and has consistently found the boys' social worker approachable and supportive. Nevertheless she needed "coaxing" to agree to the respite. She felt terrible and thought she was 'pushing the boys away as they had enough on their plate already'. It took her a full six months to feel the benefit of 'the boys being away'. Looking back, she has no doubts that the respite 'kept my sanity' and prevented her from getting too 'cranky': 'Respite care is one of the best things that has happened in the last few years. I feel I get rest. I do things I can't do when the boys are here, like go away for the weekend to stay with friends who spoil me.' Ideally Mrs. Brown would like a respite to cover a week in the summer, Easter and Christmas to enable her to go on holiday. Informal arrangements with friends and neighbours have helped, but the wider local community finds it difficult to tolerate the boys' behaviour. Steven's school considers him a "child at risk" and he cannot partake in organised school holidays. The same applies to holidays by local voluntary organisations. Amongst local clubs, Steven is only welcomed in the Boys' Brigade.

Mrs. Brown thinks highly of the Smiths describing them as 'an extension to the family'. What she finds particularly valuable is that she has been able to communicate and share with them Steven and Ken's problems, and thus lessen her sense of isolation. The fact that both families are Roman Catholic has created an important link for Mrs. Brown by allowing Steven and Ken to continue to go to Church. It has been very important for Mrs. Brown that Steven and Ken have enjoyed their visits to the Smiths. Steven has liked going to the Smiths more than Ken, but Mrs. Brown insists she would not have agreed to the respite if Ken was in any way unhappy about it. She sees the benefits of the respite for the boys as looking on the Smiths as their aunt and uncle, being able to play in open fields, having more freedom and more opportunities to engage in various activities. She is sad that the Smiths can no longer be the respite carers, but she hopes Steven and Ken will be able, if they want, to keep in touch with them during the school holidays. She is optimistic that the arrangements for respite with her friend and daughter will work well, as the boys already know them and 'they don't like change'.

References

1. Filmer A, *Family Based – A Report on a Survey of Respite Care Schemes in Scotland*, Shared Care Scotland, 1994.

2. Lindsay M, Kohls M, and Collins J, *The Patchwork Quilt – A study of respite care services in Scotland,* Social Work Inspectorate for Scotland, 1993.

3. Irving K, 'Flexitime', *Community Care*, 23–31, May 1995.

4. Bradley M, and Aldgate J, ' Family-Based Short-Term Breaks for Children in Need', in Stalker K (ed), *Breaks and Opportunities: Developments in short-term care*, Jessica Kingsley, 1995.

11 Consultation, assessment and therapy
The contribution of the child mental health team

Dr Michael Morton

Dr Michael Morton is Consultant Child Psychiatrist at Ladyfield, Dumfries. He is a member of the executive of the Scottish Medical Group of BAAF.

The child mental health team brings together a range of approaches to problems that may arise after adoption. Psychiatric studies of adopted people and their families have helped to develop understanding of the roles of nature and nurture in the origins of adult mental illness.[1] Characteristics that may be inherited can contribute to an adopted child's difficulties (for example, dyslexia in the case of Simon, described later in the chapter). In the majority of cases it is impossible to define a specific genetic explanation for a child's psychiatric disorder.[2] Biological understanding is a central part of psychiatric training and increasing knowledge may alter practice in the future.

At present, the main contribution of child mental health professionals to adoption and post-adoption practice is based upon their understanding of emotional development, and family systems function. Attention must be paid to the unique experience of the adopted child and constitutional factors must be considered, but in many cases a focus on the individual child will not lead to resolution of problems. The traditional medical model may co-exist in child psychiatric practice with a model based upon family systems theory.[3] On this basis, a child psychiatrist acting as an external consultant may be able to contribute to problem solving without necessarily making a direct intervention at the level of the individual symptom, patient, client or family. Where such consultation activity is an established aspect of child mental health services, NHS purchasing contracts need to attend to this aspect of service provision so that funding is not dependent upon a clinic model of activity focusing solely upon numbers of cases seen.[4]

Consultation is not always appropriate and there will always be children who need to be seen in the clinic and may be offered out-patient treatment, or more rarely, day-patient or in-patient assessment of therapy. There are often concerns that such children are labelled as having a child psychiatric disorder.

There is some confusion about labels as it is rare for children to develop adult-type mental illness but there are recognised patterns of emotional, behavioural, and developmental disturbance which attract descriptive labels within the international Classification of Diseases.[5] Such disorders are relatively common, occurring in between 10–20 per cent of the child population.[6] Adopted children are recognised as being at increased risk of presenting to child psychiatry clinics, and they may be more likely to present with behavioural problems, especially if adopted after the age of six months.[7] As older children with more complex problems are more frequently placed for adoption, it is probable that there will also be an increasing need for advice about psychiatric disturbance following adoption.

Child mental health services have traditionally operated within a multidisciplinary and often multiagency framework. The child mental health team may include local authority social workers and educational psychologists working alongside NHS doctors, nurses, psychologists and therapists. Regrettably, the opportunity of working within a multi-disciplinary team is not open to all psychiatrists, but policies that emphasise partnership between local authority and health service staff may offer an opportunity for reopening relationships that in some cases have been lost. The work of the child mental health team in post-adoption support depends upon collaboration with other agencies. Within my own area (Dumfries and Galloway) some progress has been achieved in this regard as a result of interagency training for senior staff in health, education, social work and the voluntary services. Joint training allows for increased mutual understanding in an area of work where limited resources and overlapping roles and responsibilities may lead both to duplication of activity and also failure to refer between agencies.

Referral and consultation

Access to child mental health services may follow referral from health, social work or education staff, according to local policy. The agenda of the referrer may differ from the expectation of the mental health team. Within a child mental health service, an assessment will be carried out before treatment can be offered. Referring agencies may struggle with this notion if referral has been made for the specific purpose of obtaining therapy for a child and family.

From the point of view of the child mental health team, the referrer's assessment will be respected but it is rarely all that will be required. The team represents a combined expertise based upon extensive experience, and it is essential that the professionals concerned should be able to assure themselves that the proposed approach will be effective and will not lead to further difficulties. Referral may lead to a consultation meeting to clarify these issues before the decision to offer an appointment to child and family.

Issues that may be clarified by consultation can arise when an adoptive parent or professional supporting a family identifies a need for a child to receive therapeutic work in order to come to terms with the experience of adoption. Behavioural disturbance on the part of the child is often the reason therapy has been requested. It is not unusual to find that the child believes that his/her adoptive placement is insecure and behavioural disturbance reflects fear of disruption. In such circumstances, it is unlikely that therapeutic work with the child alone will be successful. The primary task then is to reassure the child that the placement is secure and this may involve a painful acknowledgement of difficulties on behalf of the adults involved. A recent study[8] highlighted the finding that adoptive families are more likely to seek to resolve difficulties with a child by a solution that relies on the child staying outside the family, either in a residential setting, for example, school, or by returning to local authority care. Where such a solution is being considered this will feed in to the child's own insecurity. Such issues must be tackled before the child can feel sufficiently secure to explore his/her own feelings within a therapeutic setting (if that is still necessary).

In addition to consultation to primary care and local authority agencies, the child mental health team may offer a significant regular consultative input to child health services. Problems concerning the complex interplay of constitutional, genetic and environmental factors may arise prior to placement or subsequently within adoptive families. The child psychiatrist's task may be to alert paediatric staff to special issues in adoption and to offer advice about psychological aspects of treatment within a family systems perspective.

Assessment

In many cases the child and family will be offered an assessment appointment with one or more members of the team. At this time, expectations of the child psychiatry clinic are of great importance. Engagement is aided by preparation work with child and family. The family, who have been aware of the possibility of problems of psychological adjustment at the time of adoption, may be better prepared than those to whom referral may seem to be an indicator of failure. It is not unusual for children to arrive at the clinic with curious expectations. Sometimes the interviewer is seen as a person who will chastise the child for bad behaviour. On other occasions, unrealistic expectations of therapy lead the child to believe that by attending the clinic he or she will resolve all their fears and fantasies regarding their adoptive status. In my own practice I find it helpful at the start to emphasise the importance of achieving understanding before attempting change.

A child psychiatry approach to assessment taking account of physical medical, developmental, psychiatric and social factors, provides an opportunity for holistic understanding of the complex problems that may arise after adoption.[9] Assessment can take many forms according to the case. In some cases, a confidential individual interview or play session with the child may be the central plank of the assessment. In others, a preliminary discussion will identify the need for specific psychological testing, physical examination and investigation or a focus on aspects of functioning of other family members.

An assessment of family function is likely to be of great importance and may be contentious for adoptive families. Exploration of family functioning may lead adoptive parents to believe that they are blamed for problems in the child. In such cases it is helpful if the concept of a vicious cycle of family dysfunction can be understood. Many adoptive children bring tremendous challenges to their new families and it is not surprising that on occasions these difficulties prove to be more than the family can manage within its own resources. When support is not available at an early stage, parents' ability to cope may be undermined to the extent that depression or marital dysfunction may ensue. There is a danger that a focus on the adopted child may lead to failure to identify other important issues within the family.

A depressed parent in marital conflict is unlikely to be able to tackle the significant challenges offered by some severely disturbed adopted children. By the time that referral has been made, a vicious cycle of parental distress and child disturbance is often well established.

An important component of assessment may involve consideration of the position of the family in relation to other systems. One of the reasons for referral may be that an adoptive parent has despaired of achieving help through the placing agency. Child mental health services are the end point of requests from primary health care practitioners, GPs, health visitors, and school medical and nursing staff. In some cases, the adopted child or adoptive parent may be unable to overcome feelings about perceived past failure of local authority agencies, and the National Health Service is seen as an alternative source of support.

Therapy in context
Most of the work of child psychiatry is carried out in the out-patient setting. It is important that this is confidential and to a degree separate from other agencies. Therapy for child and family proceeds most successfully when there is full understanding of its context.

In the individual case, there is a danger that the process of seeking help may compound difficulties within the child or the family and between the agencies. A paper published in the British Journal of Medical Psychology[10] beautifully describes the dangers for the special patient who seeks help from a succession of professionals. Mental health practitioners should always be alert to the possibility that they are used as a recipient of positive emotional projections so that their involvement may sanction an equally unrealistic denigration of other agencies. This may represent pathological processes of a disturbed child or family rather than a problem in other agencies. A child's emotional privation may lead to failure to progress beyond an infantile world view where there is no ambivalence and everything is either all good or all bad. Families may become caught up in the child's disturbance to the extent that they too see the world in terms of those who are "good" (i.e. an ordinary positive comment is seen as unconditionally supportive of the child and family) or "bad" (i.e. any criticism may be seen, as if from the child's point of view, as totally rejecting and punitive).

In these circumstances, the ability of the child mental health team to sustain a relationship with other agencies will be of enormous importance. The adoptive family which insists that they have been let down repeatedly may be listened to respectfully in the child psychiatric clinic. It may take several meetings before the trust of child and parent can be obtained, to a point where reflection on the realities of past attempts at providing support to the family can confront an established world view. It is important not to undermine fellow professionals as even listening attentively may be misperceived as acceptance of family myths. It is not unusual to obtain feedback from third parties that the family believes that the child mental health team shares their view of the inadequacies of the other agencies. Other professionals need to be able to trust that they are not being denigrated by child mental health workers, and to be aware that pre-existing rivalries between agencies will be stirred up by such psychological processes. Over time the worker may succeed in challenging the family's sense of being unsupported. Permission may be sought to establish contact with other services. The boundaries of confidentiality need careful negotiation while respecting the hurt feelings of a child and family in distress. One long-term aim in such a circumstance should be the working through of such feelings so that the placing agency may be approached for help in future.

In some cases religious, racial or ethnic issues may present an additional barrier to the renegotiation of relationships between the child, the family, and the agencies. Professionals must acknowledge that cultures and class may differ in expectations of development and in explanatory models of disorder. Problems may arise as a primary result of individual or institutional racism, or as a secondary consequence of a family's understandable distrust of professional agencies. If not addressed, such issues may prevent resolution of problems in the best interests of a child within his/her own culture.

Simon, out-patient: fictional case*

Simon, a 10-year-old African-Caribbean boy with severe mixed disorder of conduct and emotions and specific reading retardation (dyslexia) was adopted into a large African-Caribbean family which had previously known him as a foster child during one of his numerous moves in and out of local authority care. Simon had experienced repeated rejections. He was adopted at the age of eight and his adoptive family soon found themselves engaged in a conflict for resources from the Education Department. The white educational psychologist and the school did their best for Simon within the existing financial constraints but the family could not accept that Simon was receiving adequate provision. For the family, the battle with education services became invested with intense feelings that originated in Simon's past experiences. Simon's awareness of the conflict compounded his problems at school.

The child mental health team became involved at the request of the school doctor and worked with Simon and his family by allowing them to express and understand their complex feelings. After three such meetings, it was possible to introduce the family to joint sessions with the child psychiatrist and a black educational psychologist, and to work towards a gradual transfer of responsibility to the education agencies.

Day-patients and in-patients
In some circumstances more intensive psychiatric involvement may be

---

*The theoretical issues illustrated by fictional case examples have arisen repeatedly in my own clinical experience in Scotland and NW England, but life histories have been combined and details modified to the extent that individuals and families are not recognisable.

required. Day patient units are available in certain areas and many child psychiatrists will have access to in-patient provision. Such facilities enable more intensive assessment and treatment options to be considered. Case examples may highlight ways in which more intensive psychiatric involvement may be of benefit.

David, day patient: fictional case

David is an eight-year-old white boy, the third child adopted by a skilled working class family. Soon after David was adopted, his adoptive mother unexpectedly became pregnant and she has a younger child, age four. David was adopted at the age of three and had a background of severe emotional neglect. He was not toilet-trained at the time of adoption, and his language and many aspects of social behaviour were severely impaired. Within the adoptive family David made great strides. Within one year, his use of language had greatly improved, his eating behaviour, bowel and bladder functions were within normal limits for his age. David had problems in adjustment to school. Within six months of entry to the school his behaviour had deteriorated severely. David was unable to negotiate relationships with other children in school and was threatened with exclusion because of aggressive behaviour.

Intensive involvement from the child psychiatrist and the educational psychologist led to some improvement, but the combination of his own low self-esteem and other children's wariness based on David's aggression in the past, led to continuing difficulties with his peer group in school and with his adoptive siblings.

David and his family were offered the opportunity of his attending the child psychiatry department as a day patient during the summer vacation. A programme of structured and unstructured group work aimed to tackle David's difficulty in relationships with other children. In addition, David and his family were involved in a behavioural programme and David continued individual play therapy that he had started as an out-patient. David appreciated the experience of attending the day unit. Within this structured setting, he was able to resolve conflicts with his peer group. Symptoms of low self-esteem diminished, and David was able to develop friendships in his own community capitalising on the gains that he had made in relationship skills. David's attendance at the day unit had an impact on the family as a whole. This was the first summer holiday, since David had joined the family, where the other family members were able to relax.

In this case, the adoptive parents had many resources for dealing with David but the family was overwhelmed by his needs. The respite and therapeutic input from psychiatric day attendance altered the balance of individual and family functioning, and enabled David to negotiate the next step of socialisation. It was recognised that there was a possibility of further difficulties in future, and David's positive experience at the unit may be drawn upon if it is necessary for him to return for further work in that setting.

One advantage of day attendance is that intensive input and respite can be achieved without separating the child from the adoptive family. Adoptive children in precarious placements may feel at risk of rejection and this is sometimes a realistic anxiety. Day attendance may be insufficient to meet the needs of the child and family and a further case illustrates the use of in-patient psychiatric treatment in circumstances where a child's disturbed behaviour exceeds a family's resources and ability to address the problems.

Kenny, in-patient: fictional case

Kenny, a 10-year-old white boy of low normal intelligence with a history of neglect and abuse, was adopted at the age of two as an only child by a professional couple. He was referred to the child psychiatry clinic because of severe behavioural disturbance with outbursts of uncontrolled aggression leading to exclusion from his primary school. He was over-active, displayed problems with attention and concentration, and showed significant underachievement in all areas of the school curriculum. At home, Kenny had always been emotionally detached but at times had intense outbursts of rage during which he put himself and others at risk. Kenny's adoptive mother was depressed and taking anti-depressant medication. The family felt vulnerable to exploration of family functioning which, in their view, might lead to a process of blaming.

At the assessment interview there were concerns that relationship difficulties between his parents may be compounding Kenny's behavioural disturbance. Intensive home-based psychological input had been tried with no effect, and the extent of Kenny's difficulties was such that an assessment admission was offered.

Kenny responded to a limited degree to the structure within the unit, and his mother's emotional state greatly improved as she was freed from the burden of his behaviour. The parents' relationship improved. At first Kenny's behaviour on visits home was the best that any family member could recall. The improvement was short lived. By the end of the six week assessment period, Kenny's parents were again despairing and adoption breakdown seemed likely. Kenny's behaviour within the unit and in the unit school was little different from that which he had shown prior to admission. During the assessment, Kenny had weekly individual non-directive sessions with an occupational therapist and she alone in the team noted some progress. At first, Kenny's play in these sessions was stereotyped and preoccupied with issues of conflict between fantasy figures. He had moved on to a more regressive and messy play with sand and water and the therapist believed that he would benefit from continuing individual work in that setting.

It was decided to offer a longer therapeutic admission to continue work on the tasks of developing behavioural control and improving relationships with peers and adults. Attempts would be made to engage Kenny more effectively in education, and the family would be offered regular appointments with a family therapist whilst individual work continued with the occupational therapist. Kenny's behaviour continued to present a major challenge within the unit for many months. His work with the occupational therapist fluctuated between stereotyped play and more regressed behaviour. Eventually it was noted that regressive messy play of the kind noted within occupational therapy was occurring in other settings. Kenny was allowed messy activities including rolling in muddy puddles and play with paints. He enjoyed becoming very dirty and the subsequent bath time. This was discussed at family appointments and Kenny was encouraged to seek support from his adoptive parents. Kenny was requiring more and more physical contact from them, both within the sessions and at home. Kenny became regressed during family work, sitting on his mother's lap sucking his thumb, whilst his parents discussed recent events in the context of his past history. Kenny's need to be cared for like a much younger child was acknowledged and the circumstances in which this was possible were identified. Gradually it became clear that this need was lessening. His behaviour was more contained, and his urge to progress in education became apparent in improved attention at school in parallel with an increasing interest in life story work conducted in family meetings. This led to a plan for a discharge with continuing support in education.

The total duration of the therapeutic admission for Kenny was approximately one year. During this time, there had been intensive individual and family work in addition to work on behavioural control and education within a structured setting. The treatment undertaken with Kenny during his admission to the in-patient unit, although less intense, is comparable to work undertaken in specialist therapeutic resources, such as the Mulberry Bush School,[11] where close attention is paid to therapeutic communication within a residential setting working with a psychoanalytic model that allows the possibility of therapeutic regression.

The psychiatric unit is not a specialist psychotherapeutic institution, and Kenny's treatment took place in a setting where other children were receiving a variety of treatments, ranging from short-term behavioural interventions through to medication as treatment for hyperactivity and psychosis. It might be argued that Kenny would have benefited from transfer to a more specialist resource where he could have received treatment and education away from a psychiatric setting. Such resources are rare, and it is arguable that the approach of the child psychiatry unit enables a child to sustain a much more frequent level of contact with the family than would have been possible from a more distant therapeutic school. Close involvement in supporting Kenny through a period of regression is likely to have deepened emotional bonds within the family.

Child psychiatric in-patient units are a limited and expensive resource with differences between units in the availability of specialist expertise.[12] In-patient beds have closed in many areas in recent years, and it is not possible for the remaining units to replace a provision traditionally provided within residential educational settings. In the majority of cases, the child psychiatry in-patient unit will provide assessment of severely disturbed children and young people. Only in a few isolated cases will assessment lead on to longer term admission. Experience in the USA suggests that economic pressures may make such long-term in-patient treatment increasingly difficult to sustain,[13] but it may be important that children are able to develop therapeutic work which begins during an assessment period. In many cases, the outcome of assessment will be identification of other resources necessary to support the child's continuing development. In some cases, the emotional issues are most important, in others underlying learning difficulties or specific psychiatric disorders requiring drug or behavioural treatment may be defined as a consequence of in-patient admission. Often a combination of approaches will be required.

In many cases the early stage of admission to the in-patient unit will have relieved tensions within the adoptive family. The aim of a planned discharge should be to avoid damage from reawakening those tensions, whilst transferring responsibility back to the family and community professionals. The continued involvement of community staff with the family during the admission may be helpful. This can counteract the in-patient child psychiatry unit's recognised tendency to "adopt" children at the expense of the child's relationships with other key figures in his or her life.[14]

Great efforts are required to avoid destructive rivalries leading to conflict between child psychiatry services and other agencies whilst retaining the separate identity of the clinic, day or residential unit.

The procedure for discharge is of great importance and at this point the relationships between the in-patient team and the professionals working within the community will be of particular relevance. Discharge planning involves negotiation between agencies, and accepting the need to tie together the timetables of the in-patient resource with the procedures of the local authority (and in some cases the voluntary agencies), that may be providing services to the child and family.

Summary

Many pressures tend to isolate child mental health services from other professionals working with adopted children. Joint clinical work and planning is of great value but a degree of separation is necessary for the child mental health team to function in consultancy to the child, family and professional system. Consultation and the range of therapeutic interventions are more likely to succeed if necessary separation is balanced by mutual understanding and respect between the agencies involved. Such relationships may be enhanced by joint commissioning through the NHS purchasing arrangements and by joint training.

References

1. Turnpenny P, and Morton M, 'Adoption Studies and the Genetics of Mental Health and Behaviour', Turnpenny P (ed), *Secrets in the Genes*, BAAF, 1995.

2. Simpson S, 'Psychiatric, Learning and Behaviour Disorders', in 1 above.

3. Treacher A, and Carpenter J, *Using Family Therapy*, Blackwell, 1984.

4. Kurtz Z, *With Health in Mind*, Action for Sick Children, 1992.

5. *The ICD 10 Classification of Mental and Behavioural Disorders*, World Health Organisation, Geneva, 1992.

6. See 4 above.

7. Offord D, Aponte J, and Cross L, 'Presenting Symptomatology of Adopted Children', *Archives of General Psychiatry*, 20: pp 110–116, 1969.

8. Cohen N, Coyne J, and Duvall J, 'Adopted and Biological Children in the Clinic, Family, Parental and Child Characteristics', *Journal of Child Psychology and Psychiatry*, 34: pp 545–562, 1993.

9. Morton M, 'Medical Advisers: The place of psychological understanding', *Adoption & Fostering*, 18:4, BAAF, 1994.

10. Maine T, 'The Ailment', *British Journal of Medical Psychology*, 30: 129–145, 1957.

11. Dockar Drysdale B, *Therapy in Child Care – Re-issues in therapy and consultation in child care*, Free Association Books, 1993.

12. Green J, 'In-patient Psychiatry Units', *Archives of Disease in Childhood*, 67: pp 1120–1123, 1992.

13. Nurcombe B, 'Goal Directed Treatment Planning and the Principle of Brief Hospitalisation', *Journal of American Academy of Child and Adolescent Psychiatry*, Special Section pp 26–30,1989, USA.

14. Palmer A, Harper G, and Rivinus T, 'The "Adoption Process" in the In-patient Treatment of Children and Adolescents,' *Journal of American Academy of Child Psychiatry*, 22: pp 286–293, 1983, USA.

12 **Psychotherapy**

Mary Boston

Mary Boston is a child psychotherapist, and was formerly Senior Tutor in Child Psychotherapy and Convenor of the Adoption and Fostering Workshop at the Tavistock Clinic, London.

Earlier in this book, the difficulties of living with children who are suffering from the long-term effects of early deprivation and abuse are described (see Section III). Why is it that good parenting and loving care are not always enough to make up for these early deprivations, and why do some adopted children appear to be doing their best to repeat the pattern of their lives and to cause further disruption of placement? Can psychoanalytic psychotherapy help adopted children in their task of adjustment to a new family by addressing the conflicts underlying the difficult behaviour they often show and by trying to modify the internal images of "bad" abandoning parents which many of them have?

These are questions being tackled in a multidisciplinary workshop on adoption and fostering at the Tavistock Clinic in London and in a research project in progress there. In this research study, 31 adopted and fostered children were rated for the degree of change or improvement after a period of one to two years' psychoanalytic psychotherapy. Twenty six were judged to have improved, 23 of them considerably. These assessments were made by therapists, researchers and parents. In contrast, seven comparable children who were assessed and recommended for therapy, but for various reasons were unable to have it, made no improvement during the two year period.[1]

Thirteen of these 31 children were adopted, six before the age of six weeks. The rest were later adoptions. All but four of the 13, including two of the babies, had had traumatic earlier histories with many moves, and most had also experienced sexual or physical as well as emotional abuse. In fact, even the four children who had had apparently straightforward early adoptions were said by the therapists to be already traumatised.

The children were referred for a great variety of problems, including wetting, soiling, aggressive, destructive or sexualised behaviour. Most had learning difficulties and problems in their relationships with parents, teachers and other children. They were beset with anxieties, and low self-esteem was frequently noted. Sometimes the complaints were of less obvious difficulties. For example, there were one or two who functioned reasonably well but were felt to be not really attached and were hard to get through to.

In spite of their traumatic histories, 11 of the 13 adopted children made considerable improvement while in therapy. In one there was no change, and another broke off treatment and ran away from home just when it seemed there might be some progress. The numbers are too small for significant comparisons to be made but the study has generated a number of hypotheses for further investigation. The degree of improvement would seem to be related to the amount of therapy: more sessions with greater frequency being better. A good back-up for therapy is also linked with improvement. With these small numbers, there was no apparent difference in the success rate between adopted and long-term fostered children, but a link between stable placement and improvement is indicated.

Interestingly enough, successful therapy was not linked to severity of pre-adoption trauma. Several of the children with horrendous backgrounds did well, whereas one child who did not respond to therapy at all was an early adopted boy with apparently no previous trauma. We do not know enough yet about what makes some children more resilient to adversity than others.

A previous study[2] of psychotherapy with severely deprived children had led to the conclusion that many damaged children struggle with inner images or representations of rejecting, cruel and abandoning parents. They feel unloved and badly treated in spite of a different current reality. This not only leads to low self-esteem but to behaviour which unconsciously tends to recreate past adverse experiences. In other words, they tend to transfer or project these bad parental images on to their new carers, making life hard for the adoptive family, and sometimes threatening disruption. We found in this early study that psychoanalytic psychotherapy could sometimes help to ameliorate these unsupporting internal parental images, and thus help deprived and damaged children to relate more realistically to their new parents and to adjust to family life.

There is some confirmation of this hypothesis in the current research series. In addition to the ratings of overall improvement, we collected descriptions of more qualitative changes in the children, their relationships, feelings and attitudes. Relationships with parents and other adults improved in all but the two failed cases, although rivalry and competitiveness with other children was often still evident. School difficulties mainly improved, but poor self-esteem remained a problem for many of the children. A surprising amount of inner change, however, was reported by the therapists in many cases even though further work was usually considered necessary. There was a tendency for increased strength and supportiveness of internal figures to be experienced after therapy, leading to greater trust, confidence and feelings of security. Our evidence suggests that even children adopted as babies may have strong images of rejecting parents and this has been borne out by other research at the Anna Freud Centre.[3]

Peter

An example of the way that psychoanalytical psychotherapy can sometimes help adopted children and their parents to overcome the effects of damaging early experiences is illustrated by a 10-year-old boy I shall call Peter, who was one of the children studied. Confidentiality is very important for children and parents receiving this sort of help and to preserve this, pseudonyms are used and some identifying details are omitted.

Peter was adopted by the Little family when he was three, after a traumatic early history, with several moves and possible abuse. Peter settled fairly well and did not display the extremes of difficult behaviour shown by some of the children in our research. But his parents were worried about his unhappiness and negative feelings about himself and thought that his insecurity and very low self-esteem were becoming worse, despite their loving care. Such symptoms were noted in many of the children in our study. Peter also had frequent aches and pains which apparently had no physical cause.

His concerned adoptive parents discussed their worries about Peter with his teacher. The teacher confirmed that his work was poor and that his behaviour in class was disruptive. He was restless and anxious, found it difficult to concentrate and distracted his class mates. Both teacher and parents felt he might be under achieving. At the suggestion of the headteacher, the parents sought help at the Tavistock Clinic.

Peter's parents were offered some interviews with a child psycho-therapist so that they could explain their worries and talk about their concerns. Meanwhile Peter was seen by an educational psychologist and later by the child psychotherapist.

The educational psychologist found Peter to be well within average range of ability, able to read and to verbalise his thoughts well. But he had difficulties with pencil control and with co-ordinating tasks and tended to respond impulsively, being very easily distracted and frustrated. He was highly self-critical but sometimes refused to stay with the tasks and could only attend for short periods of time. The psychologist observed him at school and noted he was agitated and fidgety in the classroom, tapping and kicking and leaving his desk without permission.

He seemed eager to see the child psychotherapist and "poured out" at great speed about dangerous things in stories, playing in a confused and aggressive way. The psychotherapist found it hard to have any space to think, but she felt Peter showed a longing for help and under-standing and thought he could be helped by treatment. Unfortunately, there was quite a wait for a vacancy, which Peter found hard. His parents were offered some weekly help in the meantime, and this continued when Peter was eventually able to start regular work. Mrs A, Peter's new child psychotherapist, offered him a regular time and room for his sessions, free from interruption, during which he could have her exclusive attention. She provided some small toys (little people and animals), as well as drawing and modelling materials to help him to express his feelings and fantasies. Within the firm and predictable limits of the session, he was free to talk or use the material as he wished, without direction from the therapist. Her task was to observe and listen and to try to understand Peter's communications, whether in words, play or behaviour.

Peter very quickly showed her in his play how confused he was about many things and particularly about family relationships and adoption. He said his cuddly toy felt strange because it was adopted and he wanted to clear the strange feelings out of his own head by immersion in cold water. Playing with the animals, he made the kangaroos adopt the baby chimpanzees. The impulsive, restless behaviour, observed by the psychologist and teacher, was demonstrated in the therapy sessions where its meaning could gradually be unravelled. Peter often seemed to be identified with animals, darting round as if a monkey. He was preoccupied with a pop singer, who, he said, looked like a monkey, and also with various other well known male figures. It was as if he could be endlessly guessing, in his behaviour, who his father could be (actually unknown). His birthdays occasioned upsurges of anxiety about his "real" parents. He believed that his eyes were all powerful and that he could make things "gone" by looking – possibly he felt he had done this with his original parents. He maintained that he was not born but "hatched". He appeared to see strangers as potential relatives, relating rather promiscuously to all and sundry, as if he were constantly searching for lost parents or relatives or perhaps brothers and sisters.

Particularly important in this kind of psychoanalytic psychotherapy is the way the child's evolving relationship with the therapist comes to reflect his outside relationships, coloured by past experience and expectations. At the beginning of therapy, Peter related to Mrs A in a manner more characteristic of a much younger child, making an immediate, idealised and passionate relationship with her, as if she might be a long lost mother (or fairy godmother). However, when inevitable frustrations occurred, for example, having to end sessions

or put up with holiday breaks in the treatment, Peter's earlier situations of rejection and abandonment were reawakened. A temporary
loss seemed like death to Peter. Mrs A then became a very bad mother
who was abandoning him in a selfish way. At these times, Peter would
become destructive and aggressive, possibly re-enacting the physical
abuse and disturbing events of his early years.

Firm limits were needed, but as Peter and his therapist weathered and
contained these turbulent emotions, confusions were clarified and
fantasy and reality were gradually brought together so that more
genuine trust was able to develop. As a result of this work, Peter was
gradually able to take into himself and identify with more caring,
attentive but also limit-setting adult figures. This of course enabled
him to establish better and more realistic relationships with his
adoptive parents.

He remained, however, for quite some time preoccupied with his
unknown father, considering himself a "bastard". At times he was
identified with Jesus Christ, but at others he feared his father was in
prison for some dreadful crime (abandoning him, perhaps). He was
also obsessed with various sportsmen, speculating that Mrs A's
husband might be a well known athlete!

It is easy to see the reasons for Peter's restlessness and the problems
for which he was referred. With all this turmoil in his mind and such
a chaotic inner world, Peter could hardly be expected to concentrate
on school work. His superficial and impulsive way of relating,
together with his insecurity and confusion about family relationships
and his own identity, would be bound to make it difficult for his
adoptive parents to get through to him and to feel their care was
adequate. They felt that Peter had made progress in certain areas
between the time he was adopted at three and the age of 10, particularly in his being more able to acknowledge feelings of sadness, anger
and loss and his fears of failure.

They thought Peter had moved on during this time, but not enough, and fortunately they were insightful enough to realise that they and Peter needed help. As we have seen, therapy revealed that in spite of this progress there was an inner core of confusion about family figures and relationships which had not changed fundamentally since his early years. We found this unchanged inner world even more marked in other children in our study. It was also noted that Peter had not made spontaneous improvement during the year's wait for therapy, in fact the reverse.

Working through all this pain and confusion in therapy, within firm limits, gradually enabled Peter to be more in touch with his conflicting feelings and to gain more self-control. This released him to behave more appropriately in the external world and to settle successfully in secondary school. He became more thoughtful and receptive and was able to come to a more realistic understanding and acceptance of his adoption.

Peter's therapy lasted three years and his parents thought he had improved considerably. Peter came three times a week for his sessions, though most of the children in the research study managed with once a week.

A year after finishing therapy, when he was 15, Peter was seen again by a research worker. His mother reported more arguments at home, of course common during adolescence. The improvement was thought to have continued and the research worker was impressed by Peter's composure and inner strength. She judged him to be well adjusted; this was confirmed by the scores on the various tests she gave him. Peter was also asked to evaluate his own therapy and he said it had enabled him to be more in touch with his feelings.

A PS from Peter's adoptive parents
> *It seems important to add how much help we got from our own weekly sessions, which took place during one of Peter's allotted times. As adoptive parents it feels as if we have a great deal extra to cope with, especially anxiety, disappointment and guilt. We*

really needed regular support, reassurance, and help in unravel-
ling and understanding what was happening to us all. I think it
enabled us to keep going when things were particularly difficult.
Bringing a child to therapy three times a week is really demanding
and you need to believe that it's worth it.

Where is child psychotherapy available?

Child psychotherapy is a comparatively new profession, having only
been recognised by the National Health Service since 1974. Although it
is a steadily growing profession, there are still not enough child psychotherapists to go round and more are found in the London area and home
counties, where the first training schools started. However, new training
centres are now springing up in other parts of the country such as Bristol,
Birmingham, Liverpool, Nottingham, Leeds and Scotland. In Scotland,
training is well under way under the auspices of the Scottish Institute of
Human Relations, with centres in Edinburgh and Glasgow. These centres
not only train child psychotherapists but offer seminars in therapeutic
skills to psychologists, psychiatrists, social workers and educationalists.

Most child psychotherapists work for the NHS or the public sector
and some also work privately. There is still a dearth of paid training
posts and child psychotherapists are the only health professionals who
have to finance their long and expensive training themselves, although
the government is under pressure from the Child Psychotherapy Trust
to remedy this situation. Some independent bodies such as the NSPCC
and Barnardo's employ child psychotherapists, and other charities are
beginning to recruit them as well.

Most child and family clinics accept referrals directly from parents,
teachers, social workers, GPs; others may also refer.

For further information, contact the Child Psychotherapy Trust, 21
Maresfield Gardens, London NW3 5SH, or the Association of Child
Psychotherapists, Burgh House, New End Square, London NW3 1LT.

References

1. Boston M, and Lush D, 'Can child psychotherapists predict and assess their
own work?' *Newsletter of Association of Child Psychology & Psychiatry*, May
1993.

2. Boston M, and Szur R, *Psychotherapy with Severely Deprived Children,* Karnac, May 1990.

3. Hodges J, 'Two Crucial Questions: Adopted children in psychoanalytic treatment', *Journal of Child Psychotherapy*, 10, 1984.

13 Behavioural and cognitive-behavioural approaches

Janine Roberts

Janine Roberts is Principal Clinical Psychologist, Department of Clinical Psychology, University of Manchester/Withington Hospital.

Children who have been neglected and abused, and are placed in adoptive families, remain at risk of behavioural and emotional problems which often contribute to the disruption of permanent placements. There is no single approach to the management of these difficulties. Therapists working within hospital departments of Clinical Psychology, and Child and Family Psychiatry, and also those working privately outside the NHS, have different theoretical orientations. It is also the case that different approaches suit different children at different times. Behavioural and cognitive-behavioural approaches to management are well known and widely available in the NHS. They have a sound experimental and clinical background and are acknowledged as effective ways of working with families to help children to overcome behavioural and emotional difficulties. Children are seen within the context of their family, and therapy commonly takes place over a period of two or three months with additional "top up" sessions as required.

It is a common misconception amongst parents that psychologists and psychiatrists see children on their own and use play based techniques over a period of some months or years to help children to achieve insight. Whilst this kind of approach is useful for a small number of children, it is an intensive and expensive way of working with a child and often only indicated after a period of work with the whole family. Behavioural and cognitive approaches share an emphasis on working with the child or young person as part of the family. Parents often seek treatment to bring about change in the child. By doing this, they deny their own role and that of other family members in the maintenance of problems but they also underestimate their own abilities to help the child to overcome difficulties.

Families are referred for help by their GP or social worker. There is often a marked reluctance to come forward with worries because of the implication of failure or because families feel somehow stigmatised by the referral. If they are all invited to attend they feel that they are being blamed for the problems. The same is true of a child who is seen alone. Helping a child to overcome problems has to be a collaborative venture without any implications of blame, and acknowledging that everyone has a contribution to make strengthens a fragile parent-child bond.

Behavioural approaches

Adoptive parents are often frustrated because whilst they "understand" disturbed behaviour as the result of years of disruption and neglect, they lack the tools to manage behavioural problems as they occur. Temper outbursts, soiling and smearing, bedwetting and other behaviours, may all be expressions of powerlessness and despair in the child, but if caring adults do not contain their acting out behaviour, children do not feel safe. In addition, children who lack behavioural controls are often initially unresponsive to individual and insight orientated therapy but benefit from it to work through difficult dilemmas once their behaviour is contained.

Behavioural approaches aim to provide families with the necessary tools to manage difficult behaviours. Children from deprived backgrounds often have behaviour problems resulting from previous inconsistent management and a lack of structure. Adoptive parents are faced with the task of establishing structure and behavioural limits which will foster responsibility.

The family is considered as an interactive system. The emphasis is on the relationship between the child and family and not on the child as the problem. The behaviour therapist works as consultant to the parents, assessing the child's difficulties in the new family context and advising on ways for the parents to help the child at home. In this way the clinician's role does not undermine the relationship which the parents are trying to establish.

Behavioural approaches are used to decrease undesirable behaviours such as temper tantrums, swearing, stealing, soiling and bedwetting and to increase desirable behaviours such as sharing, responding immediately to a command and using the toilet appropriately. However, children's behaviours have to be seen in a developmental context. Bed-wetting in a three-year-old is within the normal range but a parent will become worried if the child continues to wet the bed at age ten. Children entering adoptive families are often significantly developmentally delayed and any assessment of behaviour has to take this into account.

The approach emphasises a systematic analysis of the context of problems such as where they occur, with whom and at what time and aims to specify their severity in terms of how often they occur, and how long they last. There is also an analysis of the events that occur before and after the problem. The target of change is the observable behaviour and the factors that appear to maintain it now. Once a problem has been defined, families are asked to keep detailed records.

A treatment plan is devised based on "reinforcement" principles which state that positive consequences increase behaviours and negative consequences decrease behaviours. Consistency of consequences is extremely important and many adopted children have had very inconsistent and confusing management. Children differ in terms of what they find positive and negative. For some children a cuddle is very reinforcing but other children would prefer verbal praise or a "star chart". Negative consequences are also very individual – some children respond to a period of "time out" away from adults and peers while other children quite enjoy this and are more affected by a denial of privileges.

Darren

Darren was given up for adoption at the age of five. His mother had died of a drugs overdose when he was three and he had gone to live with his father and his partner and her three children. He was both sexually and physically abused in this home. After a period in foster care, he was adopted by a childless couple. He settled well initially but soon began to soil and smear faeces. His parents were referred to the Clinical Psychology department by his GP and helped to devise a behavioural programme.

They began by recording the occasions when smearing occurred, the events that preceded it, and the events which followed it. A pattern emerged which indicated that Darren would soil in response to discipline by his parents and by his school teacher. This discipline caused him great anxiety and he admitted to feeling afraid that he would be rejected. His anxiety was exacerbated by his parents' response to the soiling; they were understandably hurt and angry. Darren's adoptive parents were encouraged not to react to the soiling when it occurred but to use praise and occasional treats for appropriate use of the toilet.

They visited his school teacher who agreed not to get angry with Darren when he failed to complete work assignments but to use a positive incentive scheme in the form of a star chart. Both his parents and his teacher were encouraged to positively reinforce alternative behaviours and to ignore negative behaviours. The soiling soon resolved although Darren continued to have occasional incidents when he relapsed.

After some months, he began to remember incidents from his past and to seek an understanding of what had happened to him. He found many of his worries difficult to articulate. The psychologist involved with the family felt that now he was in a stable and secure placement, he would benefit from individual play therapy to work through some of his dilemmas; he was referred to a colleague who saw Darren over a period of two years. He remained in his adoptive family. It was acknowledged with the family that whilst Darren was now well settled, there may be times in the future when he would run into difficulties again. For example, children with a history of abuse may experience difficulties when they reach adolescence. The family were encouraged to return for further advice if needed.

Cognitive-behavioural approaches

Cognitive-behavioural approaches include a variety of strategies and procedures which all assume that faulty thinking underlies the cause of disturbance. These therapies have been used with impulsive and aggressive children who are said to lack forethought or to have thought "deficiencies" but also with older and more articulate children with affective disorders whose thinking is considered to be faulty or "distorted". All cognitive therapies have the goal of altering thinking in ways that lead to behavioural and emotional changes. The therapies share an emphasis on the role of learning in the acquisition and maintenance of behaviour, the influence of models, and the importance of environmental consequences. Secondly, they emphasise that most learning is the result of how an individual cognitively processes information.

Parents are actively encouraged to partake in any treatment, modelling their thought processes when undertaking a task, helping children to practice by role playing difficult situations, and by being involved in rewarding children for tasks.

Cognitive "deficiencies"

Work on correcting thought "deficiencies" has been largely undertaken in the USA. A review of different studies using these techniques has been put together in a valuable handbook.[1] Some children who have impulsive and/or aggressive behaviour may lack the ability to use verbal mediation and social problem solving for self-control in situations where more forethought would be helpful. The aim of therapy is to correct such "deficiencies" and to teach them to use and follow through careful, goal-directed cognitive processing.

"Self instructional training" is the most commonly described cognitive behavioural approach which aims to correct cognitive deficiencies. The general approach is described in Kendall and Braswell.[2] Children are seen in groups, and sessions involve working through a number of tasks requiring the child to choose what would come next in a sequence. These include perceptual puzzles but also role playing of problem solving in social situations. Children are trained to "stop and think" using five steps to solve problems: problem definition, problem approach, focusing attention, selecting an answer, and self praise for correct performance. Other features of the training include therapists modelling self instruction and social rewards for correct responses. In addition, children are rewarded with "chips" to exchange for prizes when they do things well, but they can also lose chips for failing to use the techniques or for going too fast.

Cognitive "distortions"

Emotional disorders such as anxiety and depression are common in adopted children. These children may be quiet and withdrawn and cause no immediate worries to their parents and consequently their problems may be overlooked. However, such problems may also be an underlying cause for behavioural difficulties. A number of different approaches based on different theoretical orientations have been used to help these children. Early authors focussed on the effects of separation and loss, and psychodynamic theory has also been influential as an explanation of behaviour and guide to intervention. Cognitive therapies are a relatively recent development. To use this approach children need to be able to express themselves and it is therefore less suitable for young or inarticulate children.

A number of cognitive approaches have been developed to treat emotional disorders in young people. They differ with respect to the specific nature of the cognitions or thoughts that they target, but share the concept that distorted thinking is central to the development and maintenance of the disorder. The focus with emotional disorders is on the treatment of thought "distortions". The task is to identify unhelpful cognitive processing, remove dysfunctional thinking patterns, and teach more adaptive strategies.

In the field of adoption and foster care, the most influential guiding theories have been based on the work of Seligman[3] and the concept of "learned helplessness". The model attributes depression to the perception of an inability to influence the outcomes in one's life or the inability to avoid negative outcomes. Seligman believes that learned helplessness results when a child's environment leads to a sense of having little or no control over rewards and punishments. More recently, the theory has been reformulated by Abrahamson et al[4] who suggest that depressed people have specific ways of thinking. They use:

    a)   internal attributions for failure, external attributions for success;

    b)   stable attributions for failure, unstable attributions for success;

    c)   global attributions for failure, specific attributions for success.

Children who enter adoptive placements have often come from chaotic backgrounds where the consequences of behaviour were unpredictable and where they felt powerless to change situations of neglect or abuse.

Their perception of causation or consequence may not be well developed or it may be developed in a distorted fashion. They may not view themselves as responsible for any action or able to produce any good effect. Or they may view themselves to be the cause of events that in reality had little to do with them. In addition, removal from home and placement elsewhere is often unwanted and beyond the control of the child. For children who attribute cause to themselves the placement confirms their view that they cannot get out of difficult situations. For children who attribute cause to others such as social workers or parents, the placement confirms their inability to influence what happens.

Using this approach, children are seen individually and their thoughts and explanations for events are examined. They are encouraged to stop thinking in the learned helplessness style which involves believing that bad events are uncontrollable, that their causes are internal or external, global and stable. In fact very few children conform exactly to the model in the ways that they think. But many do need help to sort out what consequences, both good and bad, are attributable to their own behaviour, and what can be attributed to that of others or to circumstances. The time dimension is also important. Children can be helped to understand that what happened in the past does not have to happen in the future, and also that things happen in specific contexts.

In adolescence, internal cognitive "distortions" may play a significant role in the development and maintenance of anxiety or depression and it may be possible to examine thoughts in individual therapy sessions. However, with younger children, the family environment has to be more the focus of change. In this setting, children can be helped to experience being in control of good results. For very young children, experiences such as learning to ride a bike can be used; for older children, learning how to make friends and how to please teachers.

Sarah

Sarah was a fourteen-year-old girl who was placed in long-term foster care after a history of neglect and sexual abuse. She became withdrawn and sad and lost her appetite and she was referred to the Department of Clinical Psychology by her social worker. She was seen on her own for assessment, and during the interview she was found to be significantly depressed. However, she made it clear that she would not attend further appointments, stating that she was "not mad" and didn't need anyone to talk to. Her foster carers also stated that they would not attend an appointment: they felt that their social worker was implying that they were responsible for Sarah's problems. However, they did agree to a meeting at home where they acknowledged a role in supporting Sarah to attend sessions and a need for regular review meetings to discuss progress. With their support and a clear explanation that attending the Department did not imply that she was "mad", Sarah agreed to come for a trial period because it would 'get her out of going to school'.

The first three to four sessions were spent establishing a relationship and going over her history which involved considerable periods of time spent in foster care. As she discussed her past, some of her thoughts and beliefs began to emerge. Sarah agreed to attend more sessions and to examine these in more detail. She used a diary to record times when she felt particularly bad during the week and the thoughts which accompanied these times. One example was when a friend cancelled a date because she was going clothes shopping with her mum. Sarah's thoughts were of regret that she wasn't with her own mum. She then stated that she was responsible for the break down of her family, that if she had looked after her mum and her siblings better, they would all still be together. After examining a number of such thoughts, a pattern emerged which suggested that Sarah had a fundamental belief that she had been 'born bad and stupid'and that 'nothing would ever work out' for her.

During therapy, Sarah was helped to examine her thoughts critically. For example, when discussing her thoughts about responsibility in the family, she was helped to consider alternative points of view and then to correctly attribute the family breakdown to the adults who failed to care for her and protect her. She discussed the distinction between 'doing bad things' and being a bad person and she was helped to come to terms with specific learning difficulties and enrolled in a special educational programme. She was helped to understand that this did not mean that she was 'stupid'. She was also helped to recognise and congratulate herself for situations in which she made a good attempt at things and situations in which she did things well – situations in which 'things did work out'. Her foster carers were also encouraged to actively involve themselves in pointing out times when Sarah did things well. Over a period of six months, Sarah remained in her foster placement and her mood improved. She was reassured by her foster carers that she would not have to move again.

Conclusions

Adopted children who are referred for help with behavioural and emotional difficulties are considered no differently from other children referred with such problems. The resources exist within the National Health Service to provide them with such help although these resources are stretched and waiting lists exist in many areas. However, many parents find it hard to accept a referral for psychological help and this problem is exacerbated in adoptive families where there is particular sensitivity to "failure". Referrers such as GPs and social workers have a key role in helping families to understand that a referral to Clinical Psychology or Child and Family Psychiatry does not imply that the child is "mad" or that they are "bad" parents. By seeking advice and working together with the child at an early stage, parents may prevent later difficulties and establish a more solid foundation to their relationship.

References

1. Braswell L, and Kendall P C, 'Cognitive behavioural methods with children', in *Handbook of Cognitive Behavioural Therapies*, Dobson K S (ed), Hutchinson, 1988.

2. Kendall P C, and Braswell L 'Cognitive-behavioural self-control therapy for children: a components analysis', in *Journal of Consulting & Clinical Psychology*, 50, 672–689, 1982.

3. Seligman M, *Helplessness: On depression, development and death*, Freeman, 1975, USA.

4. Abrahamson L G, Seligman M E P, and Teasdale J D, 'Learned helplessness in humans: critique and reformulation', *Journal of Abnormal Psychology*, 87, 49–74, 1978.

14 **Art therapy with adopted children**

Barbara Greenman

Barbara Greenman is a registered Art Therapist and Tutor at the School of Art Therapy, Edinburgh.

How and why can art therapy help adopted children?

I would like to firstly give some background information about an art therapy project and how it was set up; secondly, I present a description of art therapy; and thirdly, I shall discuss some of the issues of working with children and communication with their families with reference to the project, given that parents have supported the work in different ways and all parents were new to the experience of having a child participating in art therapy. Their support and understanding has been of considerable importance and it is worth looking at how this has been achieved.

Within limits of confidentiality I would like to describe my work with the children and share with you how the children pictured their worlds and how this was worked with. I shall include in this section some discussion of the theoretical issues and presuppositions about therapy, for example, that therapy enables the child to 'get the feelings out'. I shall also include some of my own thoughts about and responses to the process.

Finally, I shall discuss the work in relation to issues in post-adoption support. Is art therapy a useful 'resource'? How might parents decide whether this is an appropriate therapy for their child? How is the work to be funded? How long need the child attend? When and where is the work to take place? What support/information do parents require whilst their child is in therapy?

The project

The art therapy project commenced in autumn 1993, with funding from BAAF (derived from a BBC *Children in Need* grant) and the Central Region Adoptive Parents Support Group. The project had been discussed as a possibility within the support group sometime in advance and I, and another art therapist who was originally considered for the work but had to decline due to other commitments, met with the group; in the first instance to give a talk and case presentation, and then to discuss group work. Thus some of the parents in the support group were aware of aspects of art therapy, and others had read about it.

Three children were selected for individual art therapy comprising twenty six weekly one hour sessions after school, at family centres near to their homes. In addition, the funding covered weekly supervision with a trainee child psychotherapist who is also a very experienced art therapist, the therapist's travel expenses to the centres, three meetings with each set of parents, and if required, meetings with other professionals involved with the children. Parents were offered the option of continuing with the sessions after this period if they decided to take over funding themselves.

Three children were identified by the region's Professional Officer for Adoption and Fostering. I then met with them and their families to discuss art therapy and the proposed sessions. For the duration of the project I met with each couple about every two months. A few months after the project I met with each couple for an informal interview about the sessions, after having sent them a questionnaire beforehand. Interviews were frank and helpful, enabling us to look at the strengths and weaknesses of the project, and to think of how certain aspects could be improved should art therapy become available for other children.

Why art therapy?
Communication takes place through pictures, actions and words. Part of the therapist's task is to understand the child's communications and to enable the child to think about them. Although the expression of feeling is useful, I think that an understanding of meanings is of longer lasting importance. It is by being able to think about meanings that the child matures. To look at meanings (and by meanings I refer to the feelings, thoughts, fantasies, and reflections which a child has about him/herself) involves a degree of trust. When fears and fantasies create the sense that something about oneself is too dangerous or destructive to be seen, shared or thought about, the child is isolated and stuck in a dangerous inner world.

The children with whom I worked were between eight and eleven years of age. They had been adopted as young children and, before the age of five, had experienced separation from birth parents and been in foster care. Responses to early experiences included anger, emotional withdrawal, lack of concentration and the wish or need to be in control.

The selection of these children for art therapy was on the basis that some therapeutic intervention would be valuable before the children reached adolescence, given that adolescence can precipitate stresses and changes.

In addition to their particular histories of late adoption, the children were in the stage of development called latency. From a psychoanalytic perspective latency is conceptualised as a pause between infancy and puberty related to temporary biological cessation of the growth of the genitals. This stage is also characterised by sublimation, development in cognitive capacity, and what Wilson describes as a need for certainty: 'to defend against the uncertainty of new experience . . . and to guard against the revival of the raw infantile life that has only so recently been left behind and repressed.'[1] In effect a therapeutic intervention in latency needs to take into account both the characteristics of latency itself, with the impetus to sublimate and control, and the growth of cognitive capacity. The probability is that the child will defend against examining earlier conflicts and deprivations.

One reason for selecting art therapy with these children was based upon the children's perceived reluctance to talk about feelings. Another reason hinges upon the child's imaginative life: making images and pictures would enable the expression of their fantasies and give form to feelings about identity and self image. A third reason was the children's interest in art; it was perhaps a favoured or best subject in school or an area of enthusiasm. This is linked with the idea that the child will feel that he or she is to be given something good, for him/herself.

I would describe the particular strengths of art therapy with these children as follows:

- Engagement with material enables representation and enactment of thoughts and feelings too difficult or painful to put into words, allowing these thoughts to be communicated and recognised.
- Conflicts from an earlier stage become apparent with the chance

that these may be shared, understood and integrated.

● The sense of control, important particularly to these children, is reflected in their use of materials, where the child's choice and construction is respected.

● Relevant issues like identity, loss, destruction and reparation become apparent in imagery.

● A visible, tangible form mediates communication. The consequences of expressing, say, angry feelings within and onto a medium are not the same as directing these feelings towards and onto another person.

● Made images can be both concrete and symbolic; an example would be of an object made as a gift, something given to another, a symbolic gesture of relationship. Another example could be the art object as a symbol to bridge a break between sessions, a temporary absence.

● Play often involves the use of art materials and the child can be playful with materials. Play can take various forms, sometimes involving contest, control, enthusiastic engagement, and belief or trust that engagement with another will be rewarding. Play can be of the dreamy meditative kind when a child feels safe and protected in her/his inner world by an adult. The therapist can become part of the play but also apart, and therefore able to question what is happening.

Practice

Art therapy is not a monolithic discipline. However, recent developments within the profession and training have induced a shift in practice, bringing art therapy closer to psychotherapy. The four Postgraduate Diploma in Art Therapy Courses in Britain are now two year full-time courses, whereas until 1994, training courses were of only one year's duration full time. In addition students are required to be in personal therapy for the duration of the training course. These requirements were established by BAAT (British Association of Art Therapists).

'Art therapy is the use of art materials within the context of a psychotherapeutic relationship. The images produced provide the focus through which a patient can express and work through the issues and concerns that have brought him or her into therapy.'[2] This definition is relevant firstly because I worked, for the duration of the project, as the children's only contact with a therapist; secondly, because my theoretical orientation, which I describe as psychodynamic within the object-relations framework, was underpinned throughout by weekly supervision from a trainee child psychotherapist who is also an experienced art therapist. During supervision, both communication through the images, and framing issues interpretatively in words were considered. This would be in contrast with a situation where an art therapist works as part of a team or therapeutic community, and where the art therapy would augment other therapeutic interventions, such as verbal psychotherapy or counselling. Certain implications would follow from the model of the project when we come to look at funding and service provision, notably duration of the work, support in the form of consultation/supervision, and meeting with family and related professionals. We can also look at preventative intent of the intervention: to work with the child to establish what the difficulty is from his/her point of view and explore ways of working with this difficulty.

It follows that the difficulty perceived by the family or social workers, the difficulty which precipitates therapy in the first instance, is not necessarily the difficulty which is recognised or acknowledged by the child. With late adoption, there are fears about placements breaking down in adolescence, based upon the notion that adolescence is a time of identity crisis. For a child, being in therapy can exacerbate unconscious and unspoken fears about their own inherent personality traits which, they may believe, caused the birth parents to reject them. Therapy also brings up issues about being "good" and a split between the good, endearing, likeable aspects of self which the child has learned to present in the course of his/her experience of adoption, and the angry, greedy and fearful bits which are concealed on the premise that the adoptive family might not be strong enough, or want the child enough, to tolerate. The fear of rejection is potent.

The siblings featured significantly with these children, and it is worth mentioning that in all instances parents thought that the sessions would enable the children 'to have something for him/herself', something not shared with siblings. This suggests that in addition to thoughts about personal identity/history, the child struggles with personal identity linked with identity as a sibling. This would be an interesting area for further research. The sibling picture can be reflected in the sessions by "change of age", a play with what it might be like to be the younger or older sibling who is perhaps believed to receive more within the family. Perhaps there is the message that it is better to be younger than older. If both children come from the same birth family, and were adopted together, then their experience within the family is as a pair and this affects identity within the family. Additionally, if two siblings come from different birth families the older one may feel, in fantasy, that the second child is adopted because he/she, the first child, is not good enough. The thought that the child is "sharing" the therapist with other unknown and perhaps "more favoured" children also emerges.

Within the creative aspect of the session, the child can try out new ways of relating to materials, to images, and to the therapist. We also consider the session as a frame: from the moment the child enters the room everything is taken as a potential communication to another.

Susan

Susan is a girl of eleven and had been adopted at the age of six, following three years in foster care. Indications that art therapy could be of benefit included Susan's interest in art, her lively imagination which was felt to be split off from day-to-day living, and a certain emotional withdrawal and isolation. Susan was to move to secondary school in the next academic year, and the timing of art therapy intervention could provide a means of addressing issues before her move to a new school. She had not previously been in therapy. I worked with her over a period of eight months which included one long break.

In her first drawing Susan portrayed a little girl with a skipping rope. The rope framed an arched and protective space around the girl. The surrounding landscape was congenial. Above was a sun wearing glasses, and in the lower corner, just disappearing from the page – a car. What might the sun, with dark glasses, be seeing? And was the fleeting car someone disappearing from her life, her view? My questions about her picture elicited little response. I wondered about this image of a self-contained little girl playing on her own.

In a later session I asked Susan if she had a favourite drawing. She told me of a drawing she had made the previous year of a farm. The drawing was torn. I asked if she was sad when the drawing was destroyed. 'No,' she said, 'I knew I would do it over again.'

The pattern of being able to duplicate or remake an object was to assume different forms in subsequent sessions. Early on this took the form of an enthusiasm for making monoprints. At a later stage, following a break which had been prolonged by unforeseen circumstances, Susan began to reproduce her paintings from her class at school, thus marking a similarity between art therapy sessions and her art class – if one was not available the other would be. If the art therapy(ist) is not there seamlessly the art teacher/class will be; feelings about loss or separation need not be experienced.

Susan and the other children with whom I worked experienced art therapy as play, the pleasurable aspects of working with materials, of having a set uninterrupted time for this and the sole attention of the therapist; and therapy as work, the discomforting addressing of fears and anxieties. In some ways the approachability of art therapy renders it more difficult to negotiate a space for reflecting upon the pictures in the form of a verbal dialogue. Interpretation, the vehicle of psychotherapy, is resisted or experienced as threatening. The child can "walk away" from the picture at the point where words are introduced. Naming comes too close to the bone. In fact, in work with the children, there was often a showing of fears but a reluctance to name them.

Although it was difficult for Susan to put feelings into words, she did begin to experiment on quite a sophisticated level with different ways of relating to me. At first she initiated some familiar games and it was through these simple games that we were able to play together, with her in control of the pattern of interaction. She then went on to evolve more complex expressions which acknowledged on some level our two different points of view.

Towards the end of our sessions, her feelings began to surface and there was a change in the imagery. She made a portrait of a young girl, the face delicately made up, the twine hair carefully curled, a small necklace around her neck. The drawing adumbrated her maturing, soon to be teenage self. She and I were admiring of this work and carefully placed it in a box for safe-keeping. Upon seeing this creation in the following session she said with some disappointment that the hair had lost its curl . . . her response evoked the sense that her good experience of/memory of the image, and something of our shared pleasure in it, had faded.

I would suggest that the sequence of moving from play, assuming a known and predictable pattern, can be a preliminary step in a more complex interaction involving exploration of identity. Furthermore, it has felt important to the children to begin to be curious and get to know something about me, before or in tandem with exploring/ presenting something of their own identity. The visual idiom, with emphasis upon seeing and being seen, facilitated this process.

I felt that by the end of the eight months Susan had moved quite a distance. Both her images and her capacity to relate within the sessions were more mature. However, we did not reach a point where this was explicitly put into words. Nor did she speak about her early experiences. When it was time to decide whether to continue with sessions or stop, the parental decision to stop was based primarily upon the sense that Susan was using the sessions more in the nature of a personal art class than as therapy. This was based upon what Susan said about the sessions and the care with which she kept her images, some of which were gifts for family and friends. When I raised with Susan the possibility of continuing, her immediate response was that it might be difficult to both attend sessions and do her homework. Later she said, 'I like coming to art therapy but I don't think it is helping (changing) me.' I felt disappointed that the sessions came to an end at the point where Susan was more lively and curious in her use of them. Susan's meticulousness and invention in her actual art work can be seen as something integral to her personality as well as a developmental task, along the lines of supporting her ego. So I think the art class/art therapy distinction is not as clear cut, particularly with latency children, as one would like it to be. Latency children are struggling to achieve mastery of tasks within their experience at school, and take pleasure in doing so. However, there is a sleeper effect of therapy and thus changes occur afterwards. When interviewed several months later, her parents noted maturational changes.

Communications with parents

Discussions with parents covered various topics: communication about the project and the art therapy process, confidentiality, timing, location and duration of sessions, how therapy could be helpful to the child, and how the children were selected for art therapy.

Communication featured as very important in several ways. Parents were aware of the project and, to some extent, of art therapy. Some parents had attended a case presentation, others had read books. Parents held different views about how much information was required. For example, some thought workshops would be useful, others that this would be too much to take on board. The suggestion of a simple introductory brochure which parents could read and discuss with the therapist at first meeting seemed to me a good idea, particularly if one anticipated some questions parents were likely to have about art therapy.

Mixed views were expressed about the frequency of meetings between therapist and parents. Meetings took place every two months except in one case where meetings were less frequent. The two months option was seen as sufficient. One parent thought that more frequent meetings would raise questions in the child about why meetings took place so often. The one lesson to be learned has been that it is necessary for parents to know that their concerns are important and the therapist can be contacted between arranged meetings.

The parents raised no objections to the children being selected by a professional worker who knew the needs of all children in the area. There was some speculation and curiosity about why their children were selected rather than others. All parents felt the timing (after school hours) and location of sessions to be satisfactory. None of the parents wanted sessions during school hours for a variety of reasons.

Confidentiality was not acknowledged to be a problem per se although parents were curious about what went on in the sessions. Some children communicated more than others to their parents about the sessions and some brought work home with them. Parents found their own ways of introducing the notion of confidentiality to their children, following initial discussion about art therapy. For example, 'What goes on between you and the therapist is confidential ... be yourself,' or 'Therapy can be a place to talk/draw about feelings that you might have but don't want to talk about (with parents, because you might hurt their feelings).' I liked the way parents found their own ways of telling their children about art therapy, better than I could, because they knew their children and knew what they would be able to understand.

The duration of the project presented each family with a choice about whether to continue with the sessions or not. I found the issues around this difficult. Should art therapy become available to other children in the future, with grant funding, I would recommend that the duration of sessions be assessed by the therapist on the basis of ongoing work with each child. It seemed to me that attempts to reach a decision about ending or continuing work involved framing questions for the children such as, 'Do you feel the sessions are helping you?' or 'Do you feel any different?' I think the children found it hard to answer because of unexpressed worries about being in therapy. Also, given the disruption of the children's early experiences, six months is a comparatively short time. It is probable that in expectation of an ending after six months children protect themselves from anticipated loss. However, valuable work was done by the children within the six month period and endings were carefully discussed and thought about by parents, child and therapist.

Perhaps one of the trickiest areas to communicate about with parents is the way a child can be in touch with different ages within a session: at one moment mature, relating achievements and experiences of school life, at another time showing you what it might be like to be half their age, recalling or re-evoking early experience. Words like regression do not quite match the transitions which take place. Particularly with these children, whose early attachments were unsteady, communications about early experience can convey some of the questions, losses and speculations about their baby/younger selves. However, parents who are concerned in any case about their children's maturation and behaviour, can find indications of young childlike behaviour within sessions disturbing, fearing that the child is not using the session appropriately, or that this behaviour might spill over into life outwith the sessions.

One valued aspect of occasionally being able to be "babyish" is that issues of dependency may come up, which are particularly difficult for children who needed too early on to be independent in order to survive emotionally. Through play, presentation and representation of early experience in pictorial form, followed by reflection, there arises the possibility of the child establishing a modification of conflicts and a more secure sense of identity in the present. When fears are shown, through drawing, play and verbal expression, it is possible to address the fears together: the child is not rejected for showing more vulnerable aspects of self. This is a gradual process and it takes time to build up trust that fears can be recognised and contained. Children may present their distressed area in either an image or in actions upon an image (for example, tearing up a picture or ensuring that it be kept safely). This enactment can be explored verbally in terms of meanings with the child, if the child is ready to do so. Even if not verbally addressed quite potent meanings can be exchanged, and the child can experience some degree of being understood and known.

Art therapy in the context of post-adoption support

Work with these children suggests that art therapy can contribute to the mediation and modification of children's perceptions of self and world. It also suggests, as with most therapy interventions, that certain conditions enable the work to proceed in an optimal fashion.

● The support of parents is primary; their role is considerable, ranging from the practical task of getting the child to and from sessions to making a space for this weekly commitment within the family. On an emotional level, parents will be carrying a degree of uncertainty about the work. They seek and hope for signs of change. The sessions will, at times, raise a level of conflict within the child as fears get close to the surface, and finally, confidentiality precludes disclosure of the work within the sessions which could alleviate some parental uncertainty but at the expense of the child's privacy and working space.

● Established meetings with parents and other workers involved with the child need to be built into the work as well as the understanding that parents can contact the therapist if concerned about any aspect of the work. In some instances parents might find it useful to have some support from another worker for the feelings raised by having a child in therapy. With adoptive families having a child in art therapy can evoke, in some cases, earlier difficult experiences in the process of adoption.

● Duration of therapy is a big issue. Given the early disruption in these children's lives and the stage of latency, it takes time to develop trust. One might question the provision of ongoing therapy on grounds of cost. However, these are children with long-term needs for continuity, given that early attachments were insecure and disrupted. Parents too benefit from continuity and it takes time to build up a working relationship with families. Longer term psychodynamic therapies which deal with the working through of feelings and the testing out over time of the reliability of the sessions/therapist enable the child to assimilate experience over time. Realistically one would consider a weekly intervention of eighteen months to two years.

● The funding implications are considerable. Administratively arrangements can be made for a special allowance to the parents, who then pay the therapist for sessions with the child. I personally feel uneasy about this arrangement on several counts. The weekly payment to the therapist, if it is to include travel, probably seems an enormous amount to most families, particularly if equated with other things which could be purchased by families. Workers from statutory services provide services without families being aware of the cost. One suggestion would be to provide an allowance or payment direct to the therapist from a funding agency to provide an ongoing service for several children. Children could be put on a waiting list for assessment and taken on when a vacancy arises. If the art therapy service were linked with other therapies, eg. music, play, drama, or psychotherapy the children would reap the benefit of a co-ordinated service.

There would be a point of contact for referring agencies and the service would be thus improved.

● Supervision and consultation, in which the therapist is able to discuss the work with an experienced practitioner, is a basic requirement for good practice.

● Family centres have provided convenient and supportive venues close to the homes of children. Parents have indicated a reluctance for their children to participate in therapy during school hours. This rather limits the service. Working within this constraint is possible but from a practitioner's point of view not ideal, because of travelling time. From the practitioner's point of view work within a centre, with an art therapy room, for a day(s) would be a more attractive option.

References

1. Wilson P, 'Latency and Certainty', *Journal of Child Psychotherapy*, 15:2, p 60, 1989.

2. Dalley T, Rifkind G, and Terry K, *Three Voices of Art Therapy*, Routledge, 1993.

15 **Group play therapy**

Barbara Bennett

Barbara Bennett is a Local Authority Education Department Psychologist in Central Regional Council.

The views and opinions expressed are those of the author and do not necessarily reflect Regional policy.

When older children move into permanent placements they often do so with a history which includes difficulties in peer group relationships. At a time when the focus of planning is in relation to a new family unit, the area of peer group relationships is of lesser importance than other issues. Interactions with the new parent figures and with the other individuals within the family naturally take precedence. The issue of ongoing contact or not with a birth parent may also need to be addressed, as well as all that is involved in the process of the move and the transition from one set of carers to another. With this heavy agenda it is perhaps not surprising that how the child copes with peers at school, in organised activities or in more informal settings, is of lesser importance in the planning for the move. There is also often the hope that any problems in this area will disappear when the child knows he/she is in a permanent placement.

Whilst for some children all may go smoothly, for others things can remain problematic. This often presents in playground disagreements and fights. Fitting in with the organisation and structure of class or group out-of-school activities can also be difficult, as can sustaining play with children in the neighbourhood. When some or all of this happens, the pressures on the new family and, particularly, on the new parents is enormous. Having to do business with schools over persistent unacceptable behaviour is often a new experience. For adults who may still not feel overly confident in areas of parenting, the failure experienced in not effecting the desired change can add to insecurities and may be further added to by what they perceive as criticism of themselves, as the persons responsible for the child. Relationships with neighbours and friends can also become difficult when problems in sharing and co-operating lead to falling-outs between children. Knowing how to encourage an isolated child in participation with others when he or she seems happy with his/her own company can also be a big worry. All of this can be around despite the child showing attachments to the new key figures in his/her life and fitting into the new family in an acceptable way. It can be all the more puzzling and disappointing because of this.

When such situations arise, the "good advice" and the normal strategies have not worked. Promises are often made by the child, with great commitment at the time, but then seem to be forgotten. Problems repeat. There is an absence of learning in the child and the adults feel frustrated. Dealing with this frustration is not easy when growing relationships have to be protected. For the child there is a feeling of failure, of letting people down and, perhaps, of being "really bad" again – all reminiscent of the past. This can create anxieties which may result in an escalation of testing behaviour.

For children who display this pattern of difficulty group play therapy can be a positive intervention. Within a safe, contained setting relationships with other children can be explored through the medium of play. The opportunity to grow within themselves and in their understanding of how they can be with, and react to, other children is offered. With the interface of relationships as the major focus of the work, finding new understandings and new ways of being with others can develop. It is, of course, essential that this work is supported by all the adults in the child's life so that changes in the child's behaviour can be properly understood and responded to by those who are with the child day to day. Are the difficulties really there? Are we seeking excuses? Can things change?

Within Central Region a small number of children who have moved to new families have been able to participate in such work. They have joined a once weekly, fifty minute session, catering for three children at any time and led by one worker. With a basic but consistent selection of play materials available to them, they have found ways of being with other children that are more productive than past patterns of behaviour.

This has enabled them to live more peaceably within relationships elsewhere, with the enhanced self-confidence and self-esteem that come from such change.

With the therapist being a psychologist working for the Regional Psychological Service, the experience has been available to children identified by colleagues within the Service; in some cases children have been referred for consideration by parents who had heard of the work. If a child is accepted for the group, the referring psychologist has played a key role in the support of the work, liaising with the child's school and other professionals involved, and meeting with the child's parents on a regular basis.

Andrew

Andrew was not in the room for more than a few minutes before he gave a very good picture of his problems. He was clearly desperate to play with the two other boys present but had little idea of how to make the approach. With a grin on his face he leapt on the back of one boy. He seemed quite unaware of the inappropriateness of this action and did not allow the reaction it received to register. Although aged eight he was still at the stage where physical contact was his main mode of communication. It was not hard to see why he had problems in the school playground and why he often ended up in fights.

During his time in the group he learned to use words to make his wishes known, he learned to take note of other children's responses to him, he learned there was a place for other views and wishes as well as his own, and he learned to sustain co-operative play. Sustaining play was not easy for him. His early efforts to share with others often ended in frustrated tantrums and abandoned activities.

Progress was made when he silently withdrew from confrontation. His action of centring himself in the room, prostrate in the large sand tray and covered by a large rug, however, gave a very potent message of his struggles. This phase was then followed by a capacity to articulate his unhappiness about things not going the way he wanted. Later still, he acquired the ability to deal with confrontation through negotiation and accommodation and to enjoy the continuation of a game rich in ideas, with shared decisions and actions.

Developments in his behaviour within the group were paralleled by progress in relationships with other children in school, at home and in the community and was maintained through his transfer to the more demanding scene of secondary education.

Robert

Robert's need to follow set patterns and to do his own thing was a feature of his earliest sessions. Whilst this superficially appeared positive it also hid his difficulty in knowing how to really play and his fearfulness of involvement.

With the passage of time, he was able to relinquish the activities which had drawn him initially with their structure and superficial sophistication, and allow himself to experience the earliest stages of solitary physical play. His jumping and bouncing, safely held in the eye of the adult present, allowed him to experiment, discover and gain confidence. He was then able to develop these toddler-like activities by incorporating elements of the other children's play. A different piece of equipment, a new noise, a new action – all or some of these were copied and played with. Real co-operation then emerged, initially only briefly, but later to be sustained during substantial periods of fantasy play.

Within the sessions he was able to find a real sense of fun in play, on his own and with others, and a new capacity to use his ideas and thinking. He brought to his final sessions a richness and creativity which was in marked contrast to his early days in the group when he had complained that we had no "proper toys". He was referring to those with batteries and buttons.

David

David came to the group with reports of his great need to control the action and an inability to cope when things did not go his way. This had resulted in a lot of problems whenever he had to be with other children.

In his early sessions it was clear that he did, indeed, have a great need to determine the course of events and could exert considerable influence over others. For him the work that followed involved experiencing that he was not all powerful and that he could survive the upsets this entailed. He was then able to show great pleasure when he was part of co-operative activity where his ideas were valued but, also, where he was able to value those of others.

Using opportunities provided

For these children the experience in the group provided an opportunity that could not be offered in school or at home. Without the co-operation of school or parents, however, progress would not have been possible. But what was it about the experience that enabled the changes to happen?

For each of the children the opportunity to play in a setting which safely contained not only their actions but also their feeling was important, and the few clear rules established the boundaries. They could choose what to play with and how to use it as long as this did not result in hurt or injury to themselves, to others in the room or the room itself. Time together had to be spent in the room and they all quickly learned that this meant staying in the room, despite whatever difficulties arose. Problems could not be avoided but could be faced, tolerated and worked through with adult support. It has to be noted, however, that very often the children themselves provided the real support for each other and the impetus for change. Within a group of three, opportunities naturally presented for dealing with a situation that they all clearly found difficult to manage i.e. being the third party. Learning how to make overtures and to find a place with a twosome took time. Learning how to include another, without this threatening an established and rewarding pair activity, also took time.

And what of the adult's role? For children who have had a history of being "in trouble", and may have become used to handing this over to others to sort out, it was a new experience to find that the adult was not there to do their bidding and to take to task someone who had caused upset. It was also different to find that the adult did not automatically scold those who stepped beyond acceptable limits, but encouraged a thinking about the consequences and about alternative and more acceptable ways of continuing the activity or game. This was often a difficult role for the therapist to hold. So often the temptation was to respond to invitations to become involved or to move in on the action and control, direct, suggest, protect or rescue. It was much harder to sit on the sidelines and allow the children to do the work they needed to do, at their own pace, only intervening when this was really necessary. This was particularly hard when someone was clearly struggling with difficult feelings.

For children who have had disturbed early experiences and, perhaps, a chaotic early life, to be held exclusively in the adult's eye and mind for a substantial period of time whilst "just playing" is often a new experience. To have their presence and their experiments in play enjoyed and their worries, fears, angers and upsets recognised and contained may also be very new. To have these experiments contained in regular weekly sessions, separate from the intimacy of day-to-day relationships, has always seemed very important to the children. It has allowed the safe exposure of difficult aspects of themselves whilst protecting the important relationships at home and in school in which so much has been invested.

Group play therapy, however, is not appropriate for all children. For those whose early life experiences have left them with a fragile or damaged sense of self, individual therapy or work with the family may be more relevant. For those who are sufficiently secure within themselves to seek relationships with other children, despite difficulties in establishing and sustaining these, participation in a group for a period of one to two years can be helpful.

Whilst the work and ideas described refer to only a small number of children, the experience of working in this way has been found to be helpful to the children themselves, their families and their schools. It sits alongside the work of those closely involved in the child's life and, with their understanding of the process of therapy and its implications, is an intervention which can assist the process of integration in a new family, new school and new community.

The work described would not have been possible without the encouragement and support of the Principal Psychologist, present and past colleagues in the Regional Psychological Service, the children's schools, and the Education Department Directorate which gave permission for the children to attend sessions during their school day and provided the transport for this. The progress of the children themselves and the reports of their parents about the benefits of the work for the whole family, as well as the individual children, has confirmed my view that group play therapy is a resource which can be helpful for some adopted children.

Whilst provision of this kind could be developed within a post-adoption support service, the value of having it integrated within a wider service provision, with greater potential for group combinations, should not be underestimated. As the nature of a group and the learning experience it offers is determined by the combination of individuals, efforts must always be made to ensure a good balance in group members. Sufficient capacity for interaction and active involvement at any time is necessary, but not too much! When this is achieved the pace of change can often be marked and encouraging. Providing for three children in a therapeutic session has an added attraction when services are limited by financial constraints.

The names of the children have been changed in order to protect the confidentiality of their situations.

16 **Managing open adoption arrangements**

Kath Arton and *Irene Clark*

Kath Arton has recently retired after working for many years in the field of adoption in Renfrewshire, Fife and Central Scotland. Irene Clark is Professional Officer, Adoption and Fostering, Central Regional Social Work Services.

Both of us have many years experience as specialist workers in adoption for local authorities in Scotland. In recent years we have been increasingly involved in post-adoption support and the management of open adoption arrangements. It is not the purpose of this article to make the case for open adoption, but it is our contention that the greater the degree of openness which can be achieved in adoption arrangements, the greater the chance of the adopted person enjoying health and happiness in the long term. We use the term open adoption to mean situations where there is ongoing contact between members of the child's birth family and the child after an adoption order has been granted. This contact may be face to face or by letter, direct or via a third party. For this article we obtained the views on open adoption of birth parents, adoptive parents, adopted children and adult adopted people we have been working with. The examples we use are based on our personal experience in open adoption situations.

Planning for an open adoption

When any child is to be placed for adoption a basic requirement of the planning stage is a thorough assessment of the child's needs. This should include an assessment as to whether any degree of openness would be in the child's interests, and if so, what type of contact would be appropriate. It needs to be recognised that even at the planning stage open adoption means extra work and effort from the social workers involved. It may be more difficult to find a family which, with all the other difficulties, can cope with openness; it may present extra legal difficulties and add another dimension to life story work. It will certainly involve more active work with the birth parents. If the adoption is a complicated one, it may not be possible to negotiate arrangements for openness until after the court hearing. This will present extra difficulties, with (almost inevitably) emotions running high. But if openness is assessed as being in the child's best interest, then we need to work hard to facilitate contact, even in difficult situations.

If there is to be any degree of openness in an adoption arrangement, then it is vitally important that all parties involved in the arrangement are clear at the outset what the plan for contact is, and that they are in agreement with the plan. This can mean considerable extra work for the social workers involved, particularly with the birth parent(s). Families approved for adoption have, in some agencies, already received training on the subject of openness and have spent a considerable amount of time considering their attitude to it and what degree of openness they can cope with. This training should be an integral part of any adoption assessment. For the birth parent(s), however, it may be the first time that they have heard of open adoption arrangements, and several counselling sessions will be required to enable the birth parent(s) to understand what is being planned, why it is being planned, how they feel about it and what their role in it will be.

The birth parent(s) also needs to consider whether they will be able to keep up this contact in the longer term. In a recent case, this has entailed weekly counselling for the birth mother for some eight weeks prior to placement, to enable her to participate in an open adoption arrangement.

To ensure that all parties are aware of the proposed arrangement a written contact agreement needs to be drawn up and signed by all parties, including the social workers involved. A specimen agreement can be seen at the end of this chapter. Although this document is not legally binding, we believe that a written agreement helps everyone involved to understand what they are agreeing to, as well as indicating the commitment from the agency to supporting the contact both in the short and the long term. Adopters have indicated that they have found the agreements helpful, and that they have been reassured by the clear statement that the nature and frequency of contact can be changed at their discretion, according to their child's needs and as the child matures. For adopters this helps them feel in control of their child's future. They would be less likely to agree to contact if it could not be varied, with themselves as parents being the principal decision makers.

Third party contact – letter box arrangements

This description covers arrangements whereby annual (or biannual) letters and or photographs are exchanged between the birth family and adoptive family – via a third party – usually a member of staff of the agency who placed the child. In order for this arrangement to be facilitated over a potentially lengthy period of years, a system, preferably centralised, is required within each agency. It is clear that this is not simply an administrative/clerical task. It is our experience that most adoptive families welcome guidance in writing the letter to the birth parent(s). They are keen to give information, but are anxious not to write anything which might be hurtful to the birth parent(s). Moreover, the adopters sometimes wish to discuss their feelings about the content of the letters received from the birth parent(s), or their feelings if the birth parent(s) fails to send a letter. Following the granting of an adoption order, it has been common for contact between the birth parent(s) and their social worker to come to an end. The birth family, like the adoptive family, are likely to need support and assistance to write the contact letters, and may need counselling and advice when they hear about their child's progress in the new family.

Setting up and maintaining a letter box system in adoption then is likely to be a time consuming task, and will take many social work hours in order to facilitate the exchange of information. Some families will manage this task without much assistance, but generally some discussion and feedback is helpful to both birth and adoptive families.

Furthermore, as the child grows up he/she may wish to take a more active part in the letter exchange. This raises questions about who sees the letters, and whether they should be sealed or left unsealed so that a copy can be kept on file in case of accidental loss; the frequency of the exchange may need to be increased or decreased. If one party to the agreement ceases to co-operate with the plan then careful assessment would be needed as to the exact needs of the child. If it is felt to be important to the child then how proactive should we as social workers be to try to maintain the link? With all these potential changes, we would argue that the need for social worker contact or availability is unlikely to diminish significantly over the years.

Adoptive parents value third party contact and describe the benefits in the following ways:

'No secrets between us.'

'Keeping communication route open, with possibility of fuller information if required at any time' (eg. on medical matters);

'Keeping reality alive for the child – not fantasy.'

They see some drawbacks such as

'Reminder of the pain of the birth parent on parting with the child.'

'Feelings of guilt that you have got their child.'

In the longer term they felt that openness has many advantages for their child such as

'A full knowledge of his/her history.'

'It will make it easier for them to trace birth parents if they want to.'

'It will help us as adopters to prepare the children if they wish to meet their birth parent(s).'

The group of adopters who had the letter box system had some feelings of ongoing insecurity, but this did not seem a general worry. Their main concern was if the birth parent(s) failed to keep up the contact, or as their child matured noticing perhaps the wide gulf in social circumstances between themselves and the birth parent(s).

Face to face contact arrangements

Experience suggests that families with face to face contact are most likely to choose to have the two families meet each other, rather than to have the child taken out of the adoptive home for a meeting with the birth family. These family meetings require a substantial degree of planning and support and are usually best negotiated by a social worker who is known to both the birth and the adoptive families. This may involve a worker in a visit to the adoptive family to discuss the forthcoming meeting, a visit to the birth parent(s) to discuss the meeting, accompanying the birth parent(s) to the meeting, and acting as facilitator during the contact. Visits to both the adoptive and birth families following the contact to pick up on the feelings aroused by this event will then be necessary. Experience of such contact suggests that they work best in a relaxed social setting such as a bowling alley or local park – places where families normally go to socialise together. Moreover they are likely to occur at weekends or evenings – outside normal social work hours, with the consequent resource implications.

We became concerned that face to face contacts were being set up without knowledge of or thought about the amount of social work time that would be required on a long-term basis. One of us examined a face to face arrangement with a birth parent and birth sibling occurring four times per year. After three years of this open adoption, it still takes some 40 hours of social work time per year to facilitate the contact.

Families who are living with direct contact were asked about their feelings, the benefits and difficulties of such arrangements. A common theme was that their child was more able to share feelings about their past experiences after the meetings. Although they had found the initial, and sometimes second meeting difficult, indeed one said 'nerve racking', as the number of contacts increased they became more comfortable as they came to know the birth parents better. One adoptive mother expressed the view that before the initial meetings she had wondered what they would talk about, and had been apprehensive. But she discovered during the first meeting that 'we had one thing in common, our child, and we both found that good to talk about'. Some concerns were centred round children and the birth parents: 'the child not wanting to continue to see the birth parents,' and inevitably the fears of 'the child playing one family off against the other.'

Views from adopted children about openness are difficult to obtain given that these types of adoption have only been ongoing for a few years in the UK. But as one nine-year-old child who has continuing contact with a birth parent said, 'Having two mums is confusing to other people but not to me.'

Perhaps the greatest area of increased workload for social workers in an open adoption arrangement with face to face contact, and one that is sometimes ignored, is continuing work with the birth parent(s). The birth parent requires the same level of concern and support as the adoptive parents in an open adoption situation, and given that traditional practice is for no contact or very little contact after an adoption is granted, this obviously increases social work time commitment considerably. This can be related not only to the work previously mentioned surrounding each contact visit, but the continuing contact can allow the birth parent(s) to use the social worker in a more constructive fashion.

In one case it was many months after the adoption was granted that the birth parent was able to use the worker to assist working through some of the grief involved. This was seen as a valid use of the worker's time, necessary to enable the open adoption arrangement to continue, and entailed many additional home visits to the birth parent. This kind of work with birth parents, whether relinquishing voluntarily or losing their child through a court decision, has often not been carried through or attempted by social workers up till now – there being no statutory requirement to do so. The granting of the adoption has been seen as an end point in our work rather than as one stage in an ongoing process.

This also raises the question as to how pro-active the social worker should be in continuing to encourage birth parents to remain involved. It is clear that without good continuing support some birth parents will drop out of contact arrangements. In one situation, an access visit had been arranged, but because the birth parent was the worse for drink the visit could not go ahead. The adopters, when informed, did not take a punitive line, and readily agreed to rearrange the visit for the following week when it went ahead successfully. In another situation, the birth parent was not at home when the worker called to take them to an access visit. The worker made the decision to "search out" the parent in their town by calling at known friends' houses until the parent was found and was taken to the access visit. Clearly not all people would feel that social workers should be so pro-active in searching out the parent to attend these visits. We would argue that these visits are principally for the benefit of the child and therefore the parents' difficulties and failings should not necessarily lead to cancellation of the visit, but that every endeavour needs to be made to ensure that the visit takes place.

Conclusions

As has been illustrated, any open adoption will require considerable social work time, thought and input to set up, not only at the time of placement, but also throughout the duration of the adoption which necessarily may be for many years. This has considerable resource implications for any agency which advocates open adoption as its policy. The families in our survey were all agreed that social work support had to be ongoing to facilitate openness, or at least to be readily available if needed. The more open the arrangement, the more social work support seemed to be wanted and required to facilitate the contacts. Additional demands can arise, and initial arrangements may have to be renegotiated as circumstances change and where contact agreements have broken down. To expect a social worker in a busy child care team to continue long-term work of this type is unrealistic for open adoption. Support for open adoption requires workers with specialist skills and experience, and should be incorporated as part of the post-adoption service of all adoption agencies.

CONTACT AGREEMENT ('LETTERBOX') FOR JOHN SMITH d.o.b. 12.11.92

This agreement deals with the arrangements for contact to continue between John and his birth family after he is adopted by Mr and Mrs B. This agreement is made in good faith by all those involved. The best interests of John will be considered at all times.

It is agreed that Mr and Mrs B will send a letter and photograph of John on the first day of March every year, to Margaret Brown, Social Worker, Blank Area Office of Blank Regional Council. This letter and photograph will be forwarded to John's birth parents after they have contacted Ms Brown to indicate that they wish to receive these. They should make contact on or around 1 March each year for this purpose. It is further agreed that, if John's birth parents do not make contact and request the letter and photograph, these items will then be retained in the Department's files. The letter, at this time, will be between the adopters and the birth parents, due to John's young age.

Mr and Mrs B will be happy to receive an annual letter from

John's birth parents which should be sent to Margaret Brown at the foregoing address. It is agreed that this letter will be left unsealed so that Mr and Mrs B may read it before passing on the contents to John when he reaches an age when he can understand them.

If any of the people involved in this agreement are not satisfied with the actions of another person, they should contact Margaret Brown direct. In the unlikely event of a serious disagreement, it will be open to any person involved to request the appointment of a mediator who will be independent of any of the parties involved.

AGREEMENT

I/we agree to the contact described above.

I/we agree that all actions and plans must be in the best interests of John.

I/we agree to inform Margaret Brown, Blank Area Office, of Blank Regional Council, should I/we have any change of address. I/we agree to respect John's wishes should he want to change the terms of the agreement at any time, consistent with his interests.

I/we agree that Mr and Mrs B will act as they consider to be in John's best interests and that arrangements for contact will depend on their views.

(This agreement to be signed by adopters, birth parents and social worker.)

CONTACT AGREEMENT (FACE TO FACE) FOR SUSAN JONES d.o.b. 03.03.88

This agreement deals with the arrangements for contact to continue between Susan and her birth family after she is adopted by Mr and Mrs J Smith. This agreement is made in good faith by all those involved. The best interests of Susan will be considered at all times.

It is agreed that Susan and her adoptive family will have contact with Mary, her birth mother, four times a year, and that these meetings will normally take place at the home of Mr and Mrs

Smith and will often include outings to the local park, etc. The contacts will take place during the school holidays, ie. during the Christmas, Easter, Summer and Autumn breaks. The arrangements for these contacts will be made by Margaret Brown, Social Worker at Blank Area Office.

It is further agreed that birthday and Christmas cards will be mutually exchanged and these will be sent direct between Mary, Susan and Mr and Mrs Smith.

If any of the people involved in this agreement is not satisfied with the actions of another person, they should contact Margaret Brown direct. In the unlikely event of a serious disagreement, it will be open to any person involved to request the appointment of a mediator who will be independent of any of the parties involved.

AGREEMENT

I/we agree to the contact described above.

I/we agree all actions and plans must be in the best interests of Susan.

I/we agree to inform Margaret Brown, Blank Area Office, of Blank Regional Council, of any change of address.

I/we agree to respect Susan's wishes should she wish to change the terms of this agreement at any future time, consistent with her interests.

I/we agree that Mr and Mrs Smith will act as they consider to be in Susan's best interests, and that arrangements for contact will be dependent on their views.

(This agreement to be signed by adopters, birth mother, child and social worker.)

17 **Opening up closed adoptions**

Francesca Harris

Francesca Harris is an Adoption Counsellor on behalf of Lothian Region Social Work Department, currently based at Scottish Adoption Association, Edinburgh.

For the past eight years I have worked as an adoption counsellor on behalf of Lothian Region Department of Social Work. I am now doing this work based at Scottish Adoption Association, a voluntary adoption agency.

During this time I have continually heard what it was like growing up in a "closed adoption" situation. Adopted people, on the whole, have always known that they were adopted and are intensely loyal towards their adoptive parents but their adoption has not been a subject they have been able to discuss with their parents for fear of upsetting them. In addition, the information given to adoptive parents at the time of placement is often very sparse and although they usually pass it on to the child, it is perhaps only discussed once at the time of "telling" and never referred to again. The adopted people I have met invariably want more details than they have been given, and also wish to know what has happened to their birth parents following the adoption.

I have been involved in opening up several closed adoptions. I believe it has been helpful that I was not involved in either placing the child or assessing the adoptive parents. In fact I would recommend that this work be undertaken by someone who can be seen to be "neutral" by all the parties involved.

The request to open up a "closed" adoption can come from the birth family or the adoptive parents. The counsellor's first task is to establish the validity of the request. Is it in the child's best interests? Perhaps it will be more beneficial to the adults involved in the short term but of value to the child in the long term. Sometimes it is clear that the request is unrealistic. In one situation I was approached by a birth mother on behalf of her own mother. The children were now in their mid teens and had been adopted aged three and four. The request was that the children be reintroduced to their grandmother who had terminal cancer so that she could get to know them before she died. I could not see that the children would benefit from meeting a sick, elderly woman with whom they had no previous relationship, although it was not difficult to see why this was important to the grandmother. I suggested to her that she should write a letter to the children telling them how she felt and this would be kept for them for the future.

Assuming, therefore, that the request seems reasonable the counsellor then needs to start the mediation process, negotiating an arrangement that is acceptable to all concerned. It is important to ensure that everyone understands what the arrangement is and what is expected of them. Sometimes a signed agreement can be useful here, and there needs to be scope for the arrangement to be renegotiated, should any of the parties wish it, at any time in the future.

In an adoption situation there are, inevitably, conflicting interests and it is important that one person should take responsibility for ensuring that the arrangement is adhered to, and I think that this person has to be the counsellor. When everything is running smoothly there will be little to do, but there will be times when the counsellor has to intervene, to remind people of their part in the agreement, to renegotiate the agreement, etc. Some of the situations I have been involved with demonstrate the different roles the counsellor can have.

Kelly

I was contacted by Liz, birth mother of Kelly. Kelly was the eldest of three children; she had been physically abused by Liz, taken into care, and subsequently adopted at the age of eight. Kelly was ten when Liz wanted me to find out why she had not received the photographs she had been promised. I soon discovered that although this had been discussed with the adoptive parents, no formal arrangement had been made to allow it to happen. I went to see the adoptive parents and found that they were more than willing for there to be an exchange of information and photographs between the two families. In fact they particularly wanted Kelly to have some contact with her younger siblings as they knew how much she missed them. It was agreed by all parties that there would be an exchange once a year and that the children would also exchange cards, presents and possible letters at Christmas and birthdays. There would be no direct contact and all correspondence would go through me.

This has been working well for the last three years. It is a contact which is particularly helpful for Kelly who had become an "only child", and she now has the reassurance that her brother and sister are well. Her parents feel that at some point she may ask to meet her siblings and there is no reason why this should not happen. Kelly's adoptive parents feel quite secure with this contact and their anonymity is maintained; the birth mother is being kept in touch with her eldest daughter's progress and is in a better position to talk to her other two children about why their sister is not at home. In this instance both the adoptive parents and the birth mother wish the counsellor to remain involved. Once a year I visit the adoptive parents so that they can give me news of Kelly which I then pass on in person to the birth mother. This also has the advantage of enabling me to keep in touch with both families, and should there be a need to change the agreement or for me to do some more intensive work with either family, I shall be in a better position to assist.

Sometimes a social worker is only needed at the beginning of the contact.

Tom

Tom's birth mother had learning difficulties and her elderly mother had done much of the caring when Tom was small. The grandmother's health failed and he was received into care aged two. After some time in foster care Tom was placed for adoption, against his grandmother's wishes. She felt he should not go to strangers but rather that she should bring him up herself. Her access to him was terminated just after he went to his adoptive parents, and the adoption was subsequently granted.

When Tom was five, his grandmother got in touch with me to talk about how desperate she felt about not seeing him, and how she felt she failed him because he had been adopted. By this time she was in her early eighties. The adoptive parents were contacted and asked if they would be willing to give the grandmother some information about Tom. It soon transpired that they were agreeable. In fact they were willing to take Tom to visit his grandmother on a regular basis on the understanding that it would be a visit by the whole family, and the grandmother would not question Tom regarding his name, address or where he went to school.

The grandmother agreed to these conditions and the visits have started. Every two to three months the adoptive mother telephones the grandmother to arrange the next meeting. From Tom's point of view this is an excellent arrangement as he is going back to the house where he spent many months of his life, he is seeing again the person he was most attached to when he was small, and he is doing this with the security of his new family around him. In addition he is able to see, as his grandmother becomes older and frailer, why she was not able to bring him up herself. The adoptive parents can see the benefits of the contact for Tom but they know it will not go on for ever because of the grandmother's age. It is hardest for the grandmother: much as she enjoys the visits they are tiring and stressful and she finds it hard to watch her grandson being brought up by a family with different standards to her own, and by people with whom she would not normally have nothing in common.

Unfortunately it is not always possible to open a "closed" adoption. In one instance I was approached by a social worker on behalf of parents who had adopted the fourth child of a mother whose previous three children had also been adopted. These parents had agreed to a regular information exchange with the birth mother but also wished their daughter to grow up with knowledge of and possible contact with her siblings.

I contacted the adoptive parents of the third child; they had fostered her prior to the adoption and had met the birth parents. They were keen for contact between the sisters and agreed that initially birthday cards, Christmas cards and photographs would be exchanged and from time to time there would be meetings. In each case the adoptive parents felt comfortable with direct contact and saw no need for a social worker to be involved. The level and quality of contact will, of course, depend on how well the two families get on together, but at least the pattern will have been established and the two children will grow up knowing each other.

I wrote to the adoptive parents of the two older girls who had been placed together. They were unwilling for there to be any contact, at this stage, between their daughters and their siblings, and they were also angry at having been approached with this request. They had not told their daughters that their birth mother had had two other children and did not feel that they were ready to be given this information. Clearly these adoptive parents were motivated by protectiveness as they knew from the children themselves how they had suffered when they had been with their birth mother. However, I believe that they might have found it easier to help the children to make sense of their past if they had had some on-going information about the birth mother to discuss with the children. Not only could the children perhaps have drawn some comfort from the fact that they were not the only ones to have been adopted but also, had contact with their siblings been acceptable, they would have had the opportunity to have a positive experience with members of their birth family.

Those of us involved in post-adoption support have attempted to use the lessons we have learnt from the closed adoptions of the past by main-taining some sort of contact between the adoptive family and the birth family while the child is growing up. The hope is that this will make adoption a more satisfactory experience for all those involved. So far there is evidence that the adoptive parents and the birth family value a post-adoption service and want a counsellor to remain involved with them. What we need to find out is how the child growing up feels about it all: at what stage are they made aware of the arrangements? How closely involved are they? Do they want to be? What can they do if they are unhappy with the arrangements?

Finally, there is the whole question of resources and who should administer these contact arrangements. There is no reason why the work should not be undertaken by the social workers already involved in placing children for adoption, assessing adoptive parents and offering post-placement support. Most agencies already have skilled, specialist workers who are doing this work and it would simply be a matter of widening their remit and increasing their numbers. As suggested previously, it is helpful if the worker administering the contact arrangements has not previously been involved in the adoption, but there is no reason why this should not be possible so long as there are enough workers. Writing as a practitioner rather than a manager, I would argue that the extra expenditure on staff could be justified on the grounds that post-adoption work is a valid form of preventive social work.

18 Open adoption in a transracial context
An adoptive mother's view

Andrea Lesley

Andrea Lesley is an adoptive parent.

One fine spring morning fourteen years ago we sat in the cool office of a social worker with Leroy, our nine-year-old foster son, and for the first time met his birth mother. Surrounded by her other three children, all daughters, she looked ill at ease and harassed. We were by then some way down the adoption path and were anxiously hoping that his birth mother would give her formal consent. Leroy had lived with us for a year, after many unhappy childhood experiences, and we felt strongly that we could offer him a permanent loving home. The complication was that we were white and he was black and, although we had fostered a mixed race teenager for some years and were technically a "transracial" family, we were not unaware of the difficulties that might follow. The meeting with his birth mother was therefore not intended to be a "one off" situation to be endured and then relegated to history, but was meant to be a beginning, a renewed link with his birth family and culture, however tenuous, that would give him a bridge into a world that, despite all our best endeavours, we as white parents were not part of.

Two hours and much talking later we went into the garden behind the office for photographs – the day now had a wedding celebration air about it. While we had chatted, Leroy's birth mother had cane-rowed his long African hair and the commonplace activity (to her) of plaiting and combing had reassured both her and the children alike. Promises were exchanged. She had said that she would agree to the adoption – we had said that we would visit her once or twice a year so that she could keep in touch with Leroy. None of this was "officially" necessary. We could simply have met her and walked away. The adoption would still have taken place as the mother had long ago lost all rights to Leroy's return, and we could have ignored his birth family and concentrated on bringing him up in the best way we thought possible. We had started on a road with many twists and surprises, a road that held much joy, many privileges that other adoptive families miss, and also more than a fair share of heartaches. If we could have seen into the future, would we have done the same again?

For a while Leroy was our only child as our teenage foster son had declined the opportunity to be adopted and, after a great deal of trauma, moved on to pastures new. This happened only one year after Leroy had joined us, and whilst appreciating quality time with Leroy, we had always hoped for a larger family. So two years after Leroy came, two African Caribbean siblings were placed with us – a six-year-old girl and a three-year-old boy. As with Leroy and, indeed, as is the case with older children generally, Marita and Darren were fostered initially, "with a view to adoption". It took some time for the formalities to be completed, especially as we were at pains to spend time getting to know the birth parents and trying to build a bridge between the families. While we were waiting, one year after the arrival of Marita and Darren (and against all expectations) a baby boy was born to us. When he, Joel, was nearly seven, we completed our family by adopting an eighteen-month-old baby girl who looked white but had mixed ancestry. We were now truly a transracial family and, at a time when "same race" placements were insisted upon by all authorities, in a slightly invidious position. We consoled ourselves with the thought that we were continuing with our policy of keeping in touch with the birth families wherever possible.

Marita and Darren had been very affected not only by their apparent rejection from their birth mother, but also by an unusually poor foster placement. We knew from Leroy's experience of a simply wonderful foster family who had looked after him before he came to us, that Marita and Darren's experience was both unfortunate and not the norm. Marita's hair did not grow and she looked like a male waif. Darren was very insecure and spoke only four words. They were both frightened to do anything. Marita appeared to have no experience of how to play, having spent much of her life looking after Darren, and he had been a "cot baby" knowing little of the usual experiences most babies are lucky enough to discover. They had the same birth mother, Barbara, with whom we had been in touch from the very beginning. They each had different birth fathers, and we had met and liked Marita's father although we did not see as much of him as we did of Barbara. We knew very little about Darren's birth father although we did have a very nice photograph of him holding Darren as a baby. Barbara refused to talk about him as apparently they had lost touch. Marita's relationship with her birth mother was one of slightly wary friendship. She had as a child been blamed unfairly for the breakup of the family unit, before being taken into care at the age of four, and still had emotional scars.

The visits at that time were accompanied and closely monitored by us. We tried each school holiday, Christmas, Easter and summer to meet with Marita and Darren's first mum and family and the occasion was often festive and enjoyable. However, although we had a pleasant relationship with Barbara and had met grandma, grandad and countless uncles with various girlfriends and offspring, in all honesty we were worlds apart. We had been to their house and enjoyed Caribbean cooking while attempting rather haltingly to converse over the permanently playing TV. They had visited our house and been polite, but horrified at our close vicinity to "open country", something that we, living (as we thought) so close to London, actively enjoyed! However, we were learning to appreciate each other despite our differences. Each successive meeting enhanced the positive feeling that our children had two families rather than one, and there were both joys and difficulties to be experienced on both sides as our journey progressed.

By the time that Marita was fourteen years old, she had developed into a very beautiful girl, although she was still shy in company. Darren was then eleven and about as bumptious as most lively boys of that age. There came that summer a tremendous breakthrough for both families. An African-Caribbean cousin decided to get married in style and Barbara was asked to be one of the adult bridesmaids. To our amazement she requested that Marita be a bridesmaid too and the idea was taken up with alacrity. As one of eight bridesmaids in elaborately beautiful peach satin, Marita had to attend fittings, rehearsals and family get togethers. Initially shy and rather overwhelmed by the plethora of relations that descended on her, Marita nevertheless coped extremely well with the situation. Although nervous and a little solemn, she looked lovely on the day. We had been invited as an entire family to attend the church, reception and party afterwards. Marita had stayed with Barbara at the bride's house on the night before and watched in amazement as all the women folk prepared an enormous feast of Caribbean fish and chicken dishes. Hundreds of relatives attended, many flying over from St Lucia for the occasion. We were made very welcome and enjoyed ourselves immensely, seeing nothing of Darren all evening who, it transpired, had been taken for a long "spin" in one of his uncle's flashy cars. When we dragged our children away almost forcibly at 1.00 a.m. from the second party back at the bride and groom's flat, we had the feeling that things were just "getting going" and we were being real spoilsports!

Although invited to the wedding, Leroy (now 17) refused to attend. We were very sorry about this as we felt that it would have been a real experience for him, but we could not insist as it was neither his first family nor ours! Added to this was the fact that contact with his own first family had virtually ceased the previous year, a decision made by him and accepted by us with resignation. Visits to his birth mother and her other four children had been intermittent over the years and the tendency had become for us to initiate them. Although always pleased to see his mother and younger sisters, and of late a little brother, Leroy never developed a real friendship with her. At sixteen he appeared big, strong and reliable, and his mother showed signs of wanting to lean on him rather as she had leaned on all her boyfriends in past relationships. Leroy, unable emotionally to cope with this, backed off fairly hastily and refused to go and see the family any more. He was willing for his mother to visit us, but as she could not cope with travelling on her own, that simply did not happen. As his mum found writing difficult and the phone was more "off" than "on", after sending a card at Christmas and a home video of the last time we had met, contact ceased and has not been re-established.

I think that Leroy at that time was very angry and confused. He played heavy black rap music all the time, wore Public Enemy T-shirts and wept bitterly over his first seeing of the film about Steve Biko. But he determinedly avoided being in company with black people unless he knew them. When forced into discussion about racism or racial differences he would say that all people were the same under the skin and it didn't matter to him. Since then we have learned that he has faced a great deal of racism without telling us about it; he has always been a very private and independent person and refused to let us get involved. He recently decided to go to college, having refused the opportunity when he left school, and has made many friends of all races.

After the wedding it was as if the floodgates had opened for Marita, Darren and their first family. Offers of visits, often without us, came thick and fast. However, we proceeded warily, making sure at each stage that this was what our children wanted and that they were not being pressured into more than they could cope with. At one point Marita's first father, who had been living with his current partner for some years, invited her for the weekend. She had visited before and we had met and liked her father's partner, so we agreed. During the Saturday we had a phone call from Marita saying that she had to return for some clothes as they were going to a party. Once home, however, she burst into floods of tears. Her father, in a mistaken attempt to get to know her better, had sent his girlfriend away for the weekend and was encouraging Marita to think ahead to coming to live with him in the future. At almost sixteen and appearing very grown up, he obviously thought that she could cope. But she was very unhappy at the thought and she refused to return with him that night. We had the unpleasant task of explaining to him that he was moving too fast – and then had him in tears too! Fortunately her relationship with him survived the experience and we were glad that the opportunity had presented itself for talking through the issues.

Darren did not know his birth father and, since his mother refused to talk about it, he focused instead on his many uncles who provided more than adequate alternative black male role models. They, in turn, treated him rather like a bouncy puppy, alternately giving him treats and advice and looking after him in a slightly haphazard fashion. We were very glad of the help and advice they gave him about how to cope with being black in a predominantly white society, and they were always friendly to us on our occasional meetings. We tried to steer a delicate course between allowing him the freedom to explore these new relationships and benefit from the positive aspects, without getting into situations that we thought might lead to unpleasantness or danger.

Gradually both Marita and Darren became more independent about visiting. Darren became old enough to travel on the tube by himself and, on meeting a distant cousin of the same age at his birth mother's house, was away at weekends as often as at home. We tried to reciprocate by inviting friends and relatives back home to stay as well, but it was clear that they felt uneasy and probably too restricted in our environment. So we slowly had to accept that if Darren's first relatives were prepared to have him and that was where he wanted to be, then that was alright with us as long as we knew where he was and who he was with. Although we had a fairly normal teenage (i.e. volatile) relationship with Darren and life at home was often stormy, we were pleased that at school and amongst our friends and acquaintances he had the reputation for being moderately amenable and sometimes even charming!

At sixteen, Marita started college (though she still lived at home) and, having avoided most of the boyfriend problems at school, seemed set to pack them all into her two years there. Part of the problem had been the lack of choice of black males at her school where the sprinkling of black pupils in her year were mostly female and nearly all her friends were white. After one relationship, with a white boy whose parents refused to allow him to bring her home because of her colour, she retired into a kind of defence which took the form of having immense fun with large groups of friends rather than having single relationships. At college, deliberately chosen for its racial mix as well as for the courses offered, it was a different story. Several boyfriends later we became aware that her birth mother was meeting the boyfriends before we did! Since we had a really good relationship with Marita and had always, so we thought, welcomed any of her friends home to our house, we were a touch hurt. Gently mentioning this to her in conversation one day, Marita insisted that there was nothing meant by it and seemed surprised that we felt that way. It became evident that although Marita still had a slightly uneasy relationship with her mother, she was very influenced by the family's views, including their reflection of the conventional, albeit unfair, wisdom of the black community that whilst black males could date white females, it was not acceptable for black females to date white males. As this also seemed to be the case in some white circles, she obviously felt pressured to conform. We were sad about this for two reasons. First, although having no preferences for Marita specifically to take a black partner or a white partner (or any colour for that matter!) we did feel that prejudices on both sides were limiting her experience and choice. Secondly, we had brought her up to be very independent minded. However, we had to accept that it was Marita's choice to go along with this and that interference or pressure from us would probably make things worse.

Open adoption can, in my understanding, be any contact with an adopted child's birth family whether it be simply one meeting with the birth parents before or at some point during the child's adoption, or more ongoing contact. Our experience has been extreme in that for two of our five children the contact has opened into a very real and developing relationship for both us and our children. We are still experiencing the consequences of our initial decision all those years ago. Marita, at one week's notice, moved in with her birth mother earlier this year. We knew that she was hoping to move in with her friends and, as she was 19 and a working girl, were encouraging her to that end. Apparently her friends were unable to go through with the plan and when a room appeared at her mum's house, Marita saw it as a godsend. I had to divorce my own private feelings from the whole situation. From Marita's point of view it was ideal; nearer to her work, more freedom of movement, a less "countryfied" environment and a safe place to be. I could see clearly all those advantages and half of me was really pleased that she saw her first mother as such a friend. The other half of me was a much more complicated morass of confused feelings. Three months on I still worry but have accepted the situation and, since we both make efforts to keep communication open, the hurt is retreating.

This year also saw a tremendous boost for Darren when he discovered the whereabouts of his birth father. Despite protestations from Barbara that she had no idea where he was, the black community in her area is in fact very close knit. One of the many cousins with whom Darren spent time on his visits to Barbara came from further away and knew one of Darren's half brothers through school. Secretly he gave Darren his birth father's address. Imagine his joy when on visiting this address, without prior notice, he found that alongside the photographs of his birth father's wife and children hung a photograph of himself as a baby. Apparently the family had always known of Darren's existence and hoped one day to meet him. He was welcomed with open arms and encouraged to visit at any time. Although initially Darren was worried that our reaction might be negative, we were able to reassure him that our feelings about open adoption had not changed, despite the inevitably confusing emotions over Marita's departure, and that he had our blessing. We have since met and liked his first father and wife and keep in touch by telephone. Strangely enough, our own relationship with Darren has also improved. As he often spends time with his new-found other family it could simply be that 'absence makes the heart grow fonder'; but I honestly think that meeting his first father and finding himself wanted has been an experience that no amount of loving on our part has been able to give.

Our experience of open adoption has been very mixed. We have had many tears but also a lot of fun and interest. We had a great deal of initial "hands on" help and encouragement from the adoption society that placed the children with us and their social workers have always been on the end of a phone for us. They visited us even after the children were adopted if we needed help and support. We also found that counselling from a post-adoption society was really helpful although we went to them too late to be of assistance to our two older children.

It has been a privilege to gain insights into other cultures and lifestyles and we hope it has made us less judgemental. It has allowed the son born to us to grow up with a much wider view of issues in the world such as family relationships, racism, prejudice and the importance of the individual. We have by no means finished learning and we have a long way to go. Also, our youngest child, now six years old, is growing up in an environment of contact with first families. Her own birth mother refused to meet us and we have only limited information and photographs, but we know that the day will come when Sharleen will go beyond asking questions and the hunt will be on. We do keep in touch with her foster mother although visits are few because she lives over two hundred miles away; but the principle has been laid down in our family and we will never go back on it.

For us open adoption has become an experience beyond our wildest imaginings and we do not know what the future holds. Perhaps whoever said that 'children are not given to us, only lent for a while' knew both the pleasure of bringing up children and seeing them move on. We are fortunate to have been allowed to share our children in a very special way and we are different people for having done so. In a world where there is so much family breakdown and barriers erected between people, we have tried to bring security and love and to build bridges over the gulfs. Simply to have tried is worthwhile.

19 **Mix 'n' match**

Mohsin and Shamlah Husain

Mohsin Husain is a health visitor and Chair of the Racial Equality in Health Association (which is part of the Community Relations Council). Shamlah Husain has trained as a birth teacher with the Scottish Birth Teachers' Association.

Our son was placed with us when he was ten weeks of age. We already had two natural sons and have had another natural son since his arrival. We are of white English and Pakistani origin. Because of this mix of cultures, we felt we could offer something that would perhaps help meet the needs of those children whose background we reflect.

Once our son was placed with us, we experienced a variety of reactions which we felt were particular to a mixed race couple who have adopted a mixed race child. We asked our social worker to help us to contact other mixed race couples who had also adopted mixed race children. We felt it would be helpful to understand what the common experiences are in this situation. Unfortunately she could not provide us with any contacts.

We became friendly with another mixed race couple and had known them for several months, when quite by coincidence the topic of adoption was discussed, and both families realised that our respective sons had been adopted. Talking with them further, we realised that we shared many common experiences. We all felt that these experiences were related specifically to the issue of mixed race adoption. They also had no contact with other families in a similar situation and felt that they needed support.

The main issue for us at the time was that a mixed race adopted child should have a strong sense of identity. Both families thought that the only way to achieve this was to set up a support group for parents who are adopting or who have adopted mixed race children. We hoped through the group to provide assistance and advice to parents and their children and an opportunity for them to meet families of a similar background. It was important for the group to foster links with other independent adoption groups which would allow the sharing and exchanging of information.

Our group was established in April 1994, and is called 'MOSAIC: A Support Group for Mixed Race Adoption'. The group has received a great deal of interest from professional organisations and the media; however, contact with other families has been limited. We feel this is due to the group having a very specialist interest in adoption and as the group is entirely voluntary, publicity is limited. The group may remain small for a number of years. We hope in the future to establish social events for children and parents to meet each other, and possibly, for branches to be set up in other parts of the country so that contact with other families can be more accessible.

We decided that one of the most important ways to communicate with other families and organisations was to establish a newsletter which would be produced regularly and directed to interested parties. The newsletter consists of articles of interest to families, book reviews, updates of news and media items, and personal adoption stories from either parents or children. Contributions from children, either comments or drawings, are also encouraged. At present we have 35 members on our mailing list.

As a family we were aware of the problems of identity which any adopted child can experience, let alone the endemic racism which exists in this country, and which creates added problems of identity for a growing mixed race child. In our family we feel it is an advantage having three cultures. As well as living in Scotland, there are the Pakistani and English cultures, and for us, it is important that our children learn about the Muslim religion.

When our son was placed with us, he had already been given a Christian/Scottish name by his birth mother. In the local community which is multiracial, people continually commented or seemed surprised at our choice of name for our third son, especially as our two older sons had Muslim names. We found that we had to keep on justifying why he had a different name from another culture in comparison to his brothers. We began to realise that in the long term his identity would always be as the "adopted brother", as he would continually have to tell people why he is the only brother without a Muslim name. We were not trying to hide the fact that one of our sons was adopted, but we discovered that people's attitude to us would change once they learned this was the case. This in turn made people in the community ask very personal questions about our son, eg. 'What racial mix is he?', 'Was his father or mother the Pakistani?' Also, because of his light colouring and his Scottish name, it was often presumed that he was "white", and we would be questioned as to why we had got "him" and not an Asian or mixed race Asian child. In fact a comment was made about 'how "wrong" it was for a white Scottish child to have a black father as this could cause problems of identity!'. Because of these pressures, we decided to give our son a middle Muslim name on his amended birth certificate, and to use this middle name on a daily basis. We also felt we did not want to lose his Christian name as this would be erasing a part of his identity.

Living in a multiracial area which reflects the same ethnic background of our children has been a great advantage to the strengthening of their identity. There are many families in the community who are of mixed origin themselves and our children do not see themselves as being unusual in the area. For any mixed race child brought up in isolation away from the ethnic group of one of his/her parents, there can be potential for causing problems of identity. Experiences of racism can add further complications for a mixed race child who is also adopted. We realise that it might not always be possible to live in a multiracial area, but a child needs not just to occasionally mix with black or mixed race children socially. They need to see and have regular contact with older children, adolescents and black adults to be able to form a strong sense of identity.

This point can be illustrated in the case of an African friend of ours who went to visit a missionary teacher with whom he had contact back home. The missionary, whilst teaching in Africa, had decided to adopt a black African child and brought the child back to a rural part of Scotland. When our friend went to meet the missionary, one of the first comments this adopted African child made to our friend was to ask him if he was his uncle. This child has had no contact with black people and may be confused by thinking that any person of the same race as himself is related to him. It seems that problems of identity will occur in any black or mixed race child if all they see are white faces. It is so important to regularly see people who are a part of one's ethnic origin, and of all ages, for a confident and secure identity to emerge in a society that sees anyone who is not white in a negative light.

The relationship between siblings and parents relating to their mixed race adopted child can be another important issue, especially as they grow up together and recognise their similarities and differences. We feel it is important to get at least one of the parent's ethnic origins right when placing a mixed race child for adoption. Just because the child is from a black or minority ethnic background does not mean that placing him or her with a parent of any black or minority ethnic background, will result in a successful long-term adoption that is in the interest of the child. The two examples that we can quote are our own personal experiences and that of the other mixed race couple who founded the group. In our case, we happened to be in conversation with an African Caribbean adoption social worker from England, who wanted to know if we were "interested" in a Hindu baby as one of us is Asian. What this social worker failed to understand was that apart from being Asian and the same colour, there is nothing in the background that the father and child would be able to relate to (Hindu Asians have a very different culture and language to Muslim Asians), let alone having anything in common with the adoptive mother. Would a white/British Jewish child be placed with a white/British Catholic family just because the common factor is white/British? We are well aware that we do not live in an ideal world, but it is important to get at least one of the parent's ethnic origins right, based on a common ethnic religious and cultural group.

The other family related a case where they were to be matched to a mixed race Scottish/Christian and Ethiopian child. The family had already adopted a child that was the same ethnic mix and religion (Muslim) as them. However, the only common factor this time would have been skin colour, even though racially the proposed matched child would look in no way similar to his other adopted sibling or share the family's religion, and have nothing in common with either of the parents.

We also experienced a certain degree of hostility which not only surprised us but was unexpected. The hostility took two forms. The first hostile comment we experienced was that because we already had children, to have adopted as well was unfair on infertile couples who would lose out. A few people said that we had no right to an adopted child as an infertile couple in all cases would be more deserving. We felt very much that the general public see the healthy newborn baby up for adoption as a commodity; the debate seems to be about who has the right to a child, and not the child having the right to an appropriate family. We were in effect being accused, among other things, of being "greedy". The impression they left us with was that they felt somewhat offended. Perhaps if we had adopted an older child, or a child with special needs, they would not have been so negative towards us. We would then be seen to have made some sort of personal sacrifice. After all, we must surely think we are "wonderful" to be approved to adopt a healthy newborn baby, even though we already have two natural children!

These same couples commented (to us) that they had thought of adopting in the past. However, when pressed further whether they had done anything about it, they said they had not. Was this their way of telling us that they are just as good parents as we are? Adoption is a topic which evokes very strong and deep feelings in everyone.

The second hostile reaction was regarding the race issue. Most people are aware that a family who already have children, are rarely approved to adopt a newborn baby. Many people felt that we had only been approved because of our race, not believing that we also had to go through the same procedure as any other white couple. In fact on a radio discussion, it was publicly stated that too many black and mixed race couples are now approved just on their race and not on their merit. In private the producer of the programme summed it up in a phrase when she said that the reason why many white people become upset about the race issue in adoption, is that they now see black and mixed race couples "queue jumping"; which nicely brings us back to the original concept of newborn babies for adoption being seen as commodities.

Many white people have stated to us, and we have often heard in the media, that race should never be an issue in adoption: that adoption should always be "colour blind". We have been told recently that a young child does not need to know about race, and that at such a young age children will be brain-washed. The only thing important at this stage in a child's development is love. This ignores the fact that a black or mixed race child living in a racist society will grow up with the race issue as a part of their development. After all, no matter how loving a white family is, they cannot exist in a vacuum. The pressures of a racist society will impact on the child's social development as he/she grows up.

White people make these statements from a position of power, not understanding what it is like to be discriminated against on the ground of race or colour, and when this is said to them it is not understood. Often we are told that 'love will conquer all', but when questioned if they would approve of a white child being brought up by a black parent or parents, they appeared to be uncomfortable and could not give an answer. The argument that is often used by people to discredit any one who believes in same race placement, is that this politically correct dogma would sooner see the "thousands" of black and mixed race children left in institutions instead of being adopted by caring white couples.

We believe that in all circumstances same race placement should always be aimed at, and this includes matching the child's ethnic groups with the parents' ethnic groups and not just matched on the basis of colour.

Having spoken to mixed race couples who have adopted mixed race children, social workers tend to make a big point of describing in detail the colouring of the mixed race child. The comment to us after the initial description of our son's history and background was that he "looks white". We feel that social workers are reflecting society's attitude to race and colour, in that the nearer to white the child is, it will be more acceptable to the family and therefore society. In our case, the social worker's comment meant that instead of just imagining a baby that we could love and nurture as he grew up, we also tried to imagine a half Pakistani and half Scottish baby and how "white" he would be! We felt that this was slightly distracting us from the shock that all would-be adoptors feel when they are matched with a baby. The colour of the baby had never occurred to us during our assessment and we wondered if this was a normal part of the procedure in describing the matched baby. The tone of the social worker was very much that "thankfully he is white" and weren't we "lucky" in being matched to a white baby. It made us wonder how she would have described our son had his skin colouring and features looked "typically Pakistani".

The reverse happened to another couple we knew. When they were informed they had been matched, their baby's colour was also described as being "white". They then spent the next few days imagining a white newborn baby, only to discover on the day of placement that in fact he looked like a child with typically Asiatic features and skin tone. Again this couple informed us that it had not occurred to them whilst being assessed to imagine the colour of the intended baby they wished to adopt.

We all felt it was almost as if the social workers were subconsciously trying to "sell" our children to us: that it is of merit to be "white". In fact, because colour was not an issue for us, to suddenly find we were thinking about it and trying to picture what colour a child may be like, was quite a confusing experience. The colour of the mixed race child should not be made an issue. At this sensitive stage, we feel it is important that discussion regarding skin tone and racial features should take place from the beginning of the assessment procedure.

As any mixed race family knows, their children may resemble either parent and take varying degrees of either parent's skin tone: so, when there is more than one child in the family, some may look more "black" and some more "white". Social workers really need to look long and hard at their attitudes to the colour issue in adoption. We are, however, encouraged by the positive attitude shown by many social work departments in attempting to match the needs of the mixed race child's ethnic origins to families who reflect his or her background.

The setting up of the support group for mixed race adoption has resulted in an interest shown from families and professional organisations. Many have stated that the group has opened up the subject on mixed race adoption. Most comments have been that the group has allowed people to explore the issues as there appears to have never been a group like this before. When we adopted our son, we were well aware of the fact that we will have to help him understand why he was adopted and all the feelings that he will experience growing up with that knowledge. In our naïvety, we did not expect so many other issues, least of all hostility and racism, to be part of the post adoption experience. The establishment of the group has meant that we have had an opportunity to share many experiences with others in similar situations to ourselves and this has helped to make the adoption of our son a wonderful experience for all the family.

20 Post-adoption issues in transracial adoption and same race placements

Mary Hayes

Mary Hayes is an advanced Senior Practitioner with the Independent Adoption Service in London.

This chapter addresses how, in the present climate of controversy about black issues in adoption, an effective post-adoption service can be offered to black children in white adoptive families and black children in same race placements. Additionally, it looks at how best to ensure that the long-term issues of a child's race and cultural needs are fully addressed.

Theoretically, transracial adoptions are a thing of the past, or so we were led to believe especially following the implementation of the Children Act 1989. Unfortunately, we now know that this is not the case. Black children and children of mixed parentage are still being placed in white families, often for short-term or emergency fostering. Sadly, some naive or overworked social workers tend to overlook or disregard the guidance of the Children Act when such placements are made. A number of high profile cases continue to make headlines in which white foster carers have fought to adopt the black child they were entrusted to foster short-term, until an appropriate permanent family was sought. Consequently, many of the short-term transracial foster placements have actually led to the insidious erosion of the 1989 Children Act's guidelines.

The placement of black children
Many mistakes have been made in the past regarding the placement of black children and other children of colour. First it was the "melting pot" concept, ie. we are all the same and by adopting a black child the white families were seen to be non-racist. Secondly, black families were overlooked as potential adopters because the image of all black people was tarnished for many of the insular social workers who removed black

children from their troubled families in the first place. Consequently, when committed black people came forward to adopt black children, they were rejected, discouraged or overlooked. The black families who came forward in those early days to adopt were small in number, because the majority of black families who had a genuine desire to adopt "their own" were under the impression that adoption was for white, married, middle class families only, and to some extent their interpretation of the messages was correct. It was not until black social workers and supportive white social workers convinced black people that they too were needed and could foster and adopt, that the myth of having to be white, married and middle class, was dispelled.

The Independent Adoption Service (IAS) where I am employed is a small interracial agency. IAS has been committed to same race placement for many years. The post-adoption team was initiated in 1986 with one staff member. It soon became obvious that a black member for this team was necessary, given the number of transracial adoptions made earlier in that decade. I joined the agency in 1987. My colleague had already introduced herself and the new service to our many adopters, and a newsletter was in place. The philosophy at IAS is that adopters need to have a working relationship with the adoption agency, in addition to the relationship they have formed with the assessing social worker. We have found that in order to ensure that an effective post-adoption service is being offered, adopters need to know just what a post-adoption service can provide.

For the past twenty years IAS has kept in contact with as many of our adoptive families as possible. The service has held an annual summer party inviting our transracial adopters and their children and providing an opportunity for parents to socialise and share any concerns they may have in common regarding the best or appropriate care for their black adopted child. These fun-filled events enable transracial adopters to make contact on an annual basis with the staff at IAS, both black and white, and with black families who have also adopted through IAS over the years.

Providing support to transracial families
With the development of the post-adoption team, a more formal support

system is in place. We provide support to our transracial families through home visits and workshops. By supporting the families who request assistance, my colleague and I maintain the philosophy that as the placing agency, we are available to provide support whenever we can. When families contact us, it is because issues have arisen in the family, disrupting the harmony they once experienced. Issues such as violent behaviour, or sexualised behaviour, naturally cause adopters great concern. Either my colleague or I will make a home visit in order to see first hand the family setting and to speak with family members in the comfort of their own home. The less serious issues can be dealt with in the home by the social worker. More serious problems may require additional professional help in which case appropriate referrals are made. Often the parent/s need guidance on how to talk to their child about some change in their behaviour. Sometimes the child needs to talk to someone about their birth parent/s but feels unable to raise the subject with their adopters for fear it might upset them. When it is a transracial family, the issue is often centred around race, so it is appropriate for me as the black team member to make contact. Sometimes the issue of race is a concern voiced by a parent i.e. their black child is at a stage of avoidance; not wanting to be black or wanting to be seen as black. This is not uncommon for the isolated black child. Unfortunately, not many white parents are astute enough to interpret the signs.

Within the first two years of creating the Post-Adoption Team, we wrote to our transracial adopters inviting them to a session which would allow them to raise issues they felt existed in their transracial family – things they had identified or not identified as the case may be, and differences or difficult/painful encounters which left them feeling at a loss or less capable of handling. As is often the case, those families who attended the workshops were among the best informed, or had made themselves aware of the issues or difficulties of their children's experiences. Additionally, these children were generally quite aware of who they were. They had a sense of pride in their heritage and knew, for example, which island their black parent came from. These children were given books and read books written by and about black people. Discussions at home were open regarding race, and parents had no difficulty taking their child into a black barber shop or to a black hairdresser. They had recognised the differences in their child's hair texture and skin care needs. They made themselves aware of the grooming aids their child needed and had been supplying them and applying them. These parents did not transcend their black child's identity, culture or heritage. They did not make their adopted child their "project", something a number of children felt they ultimately became. Furthermore, they did not move to rural England after the adoption order was made, thereby minimising contact with black people, and maximising the damage and isolation so many other transracially adopted children experience. Their children know they are black, or black of mixed parentage. They know that racism is real, and that being raised in a white family will not affect their status as a black person.

We already know about the damage done to some of the youngsters who were transracially adopted in the past because the placement broke down or external help was sought. Many of the transracially adopted young people are now old enough to seek help. Many of these youngsters open their hearts to me and recount the pain they have experienced – pain their loving parents were totally oblivious to. They speak of parents who misinterpreted behaviour, for example, believing that children spending all free time alone, rather than playing outside or mingling with the family after their evening meal, were conscientiously studying. Some black children were in fact mistreated, especially where there were white birth children in the family. One or two black children I have spoken to say they were treated as servants. These young people could not wait to leave home at 16 or 17. Conversely, some white adopters refused to see their child as black. They "transcended" their child's colour, culture and race, raising their adopted child as white thereby denying the difference, whether obvious or not.

This is not to say that some same race placements do not also fail or have great difficulty, whether the child is in a black or white same race family. Issues of violence, extreme anger, sexualised behaviour, sibling rivalry, stealing, etc. are not confined to one race or culture. These issues are endemic throughout society regardless of race, class or gender. The significant difference in the failure of same race placements compared to transracial placements is the concept of confusion over racial identity which often leads to a negative regard for the child's own racial group. This often manifests itself in self hate.

It goes without saying that a number of mistakes were made in the early days of adoption. Black prospective adopters were overlooked and white people who were welcomed were not adequately assessed on their understanding or their own degree of personal racism. Fortunately, not all white people who transracially adopted were racist, but a good many were. This is not to say that all of the black families who were assessed to adopt or foster black children proved to be appropriate candidates either. There was a sense of over-zealousness in order to make right the wrongs previously made.

It is to be hoped that today's black children of mixed parentage who are placed with mixed race couples will have less traumatic life experiences than those who were transracially adopted in the 1960s and 70s. For many it is still too early to ascertain the damage caused by identity confusion often as the result of transracial placements. However, in the 1990s, when we still have a high percentage of mixed parentage children requiring substitute care, social workers can be too eager to embrace partners of mixed race who come forward to adopt, simply because they are a mixed race couple. Too many children, because they are of mixed parentage, are viewed by their white adopters as white. The child's natural curiosity about his or her skin colour and difference in hair texture, etc. are seldom, if ever, satisfied by their white adopters, simply because they have been unable to handle the questions or queries raised by their black child. There is a danger that once again common assumptions will go unchallenged if social workers, both black and white, do not explore the issues of race and identity which are crucial to a child's emotional development. The very issues of race, culture and identity which were completely overlooked as key components in the assessment of white carers three decades ago must be at the centre of today's adoption assessment and training.

Black children of mixed parentage cannot afford to have the same or similar mistakes made simply because the prospective adopters reflect the child's race and culture. Social workers need more than vague assumptions. They need to feel secure with the knowledge they gather that the adopters, no matter what their racial origins, are capable of sustaining and building the child's positive sense of self-worth.

Perhaps if those earlier families and social workers had the benefit of hindsight they would have raised these issues and done something about the developing problems before they became a crisis, which may have prevented the painful breakdown of transracial adoptions.

Perhaps if they had been warned that the isolation of a black child, in a country village where there are no other black people, would at some point in the child's life create problems, the placement may have survived.

Perhaps if they were warned that life in an all-white school for the one black child would be damaging to his/her sense of who they were, the placement may have survived.

Perhaps if they had been trained to listen to their child and had done something about the negative experiences their child would ultimately experience, possibly every day, the placement may have survived.

Perhaps if they had been encouraged to interact with black people, visit black barber shops in the inner city, or experience black theatre, the placement may have survived.

Perhaps if they had been trained to learn something about their black child's culture and to incorporate them into their family culture, the placement may have survived.

Perhaps if they had been taught to look at and pay more attention to the child's needs, instead of their own needs, the placement may have survived.

The Post-Adoption Team has discovered that many white parents were understanding, sensitive and aware of racism, and as a result, their relationship with their child is strong and healthy. These parents are able to support their child and when they approach or reach their 18th birthday, encourage them in their search for their birth parents. Some adopters encourage contact with their child's birth family long before the age of consent. Many of the young black adults I see initially are beginning their search for birth parents; however, many need to talk about the confusion they have about racial identity. Fortunately, most of the young people find they can speak with me about the negative experiences they had in their "loving" adoptive homes.

Having met with black – mostly male – youngsters, I realised just how similar and painful their life experiences have been. At a glance

181

one sees a handsome, well mannered, and very polite young man. He is often well educated and gainfully employed. How wonderful, one might think initially. But after delving just below the surface, one is able to feel rather than hear the pain these young men carry around with them. Deprivation is what comes to mind: deprivation, confusion, and loneliness. Many have said in private, on separate occasions, just how they became a recluse.

Unable to share thoughts, feelings or even events at school, these youngsters would hibernate into the sanctuary of their bedroom. Most would be perceived as having all of the material things which bring so called happiness, and yet these youngsters were lonely, angry and confused. Their confusion is expressed in many ways; here is one:

What is the source of my confusion
What causes me distress
I feel that I'm an illusion, and yet
I've "been denied nothing"

My mirrors always lied to me
They told not what I saw
My parent's truth came shining through
I know now they knew the score

But now I'm grown and done it all
from college to the "job"
My parents are so proud of me
But I am still unsure – of who and what I really am
or what life has in store

I don't look like those who raised me
I don't look like those who stare
Those mirrors in my childhood
I now know they did not lie
But for love of them
I had to keep my feelings deep inside.

And now that I'm grown, forever alone
I'm almost always on my own
Can't talk to them or relate to those
What a solitary life I've chosen, but did I choose
or was it all imposed.

I'd like to fit in somewhere snug
I'd like to give myself a hug
I'd like to know where I went wrong
so that no one else repeats my song

Mary Mac

21 Transracial adopted people's support group

Mary Hayes

Mary Hayes is an advanced Senior Practitioner with the Independent Adoption Service in London.

My colleague and I established a support group for young adopted people interested in searching for their birth families. The group was predominantly white. As more and more black adopted people were reaching the age of consent, many came forward as their desire to search for their birth parents increased. We found that with a few exceptions, the black adopted people would attend only one session. It was soon clear that the original group was limited in meeting their needs.

For the most part a good many of the young adopted people's needs or issues are the same – all are searching for answers to 'Who am I?', 'Who do I look like?' So in essence they all have concerns and curiosity about identity. However, for the majority of black young people who were transracially adopted, issues of identity, racial awareness and racial pride are far more pivotal.

We decided to arrange a black-only session, recognising that some of those issues and needs were not being addressed in the predominantly white group. Letters were sent to seven young black adopted people. All but two were of mixed parentage. All had been transracially adopted with the exception of one person. They all attended the first session, and one adopted person, having sought both my permission and the group's, brought two friends, both of mixed parentage, with him. The proposed three hour meeting lasted five hours and with the exception of one individual, they all had a lot to share. For over half, this was the first time they had had an opportunity to speak with other black young people of mixed parentage who were also transracially adopted.

The session was lively and there was a sense of being overwhelmed. Some talked about feeling isolated, about being the only black person not only in the family but also in the school, church and greater community. A big problem for those living in isolated areas was the lack of mirror images – no one to model themselves after. The feelings of isolation in school, being called ugly names, forced some of them into becoming bullies, not having any other coping skills. They did not know how else to respond to the insults and the feelings aroused when racially attacked, usually verbally, often within their home, by so called loved ones. Words like "paki", "nigger" and "wog" were not uncommon as parents reflected on events in their day, over the evening meal.

Other issues raised included: being treated differently from the white "grandchildren" by the white grandparents: 'Knowing that it is your colour that is the only difference and being denied or mistreated because of this,' or 'feeling the need to latch onto the one or two black people you encounter in your life'. Conversely, 'feeling the need to hide from the only other black person in your school for fear of heightening your own difference,' and 'feeling white and not having any need to seek out the black parent/roots/ connection!' Some wanted to know if they could get information, pictures, etc, of birth parents without having to meet them face to face.

Young people raised within the Inner London area appeared to have less problems with their racial identity. One young woman said she was raised to be proud of the fact that she is black, that (her white adopters) provided opportunities for this to happen, ie. contact with black people, literature, video, plays and films of positive black role models. However, even with all of this, she never wanted both her parents taking her places at the same time. For example, on parents' evening at school she would ask one of them to stay at home. This way she could hide two things: that she was transracially adopted and that she was an adopted child. When she invited friends home, she would ponder how and when to tell them that she was adopted by white parents – she would blurt it out as the friend was entering her home.

Another adopted person said she envied her older siblings, the birth children, because they fitted so well into the family. She and her younger adopted black brother obviously did not. She said, 'I always stood out, whether I was with my family or not,' and 'I was the only person of colour in my village.' When her friends got excited about summer time and summer holidays, eager to lie in the sun to get their temporary tan, 'I resisted as much as possible, often covering myself up because I did not want to get any browner – I wanted to be less brown so that I would fit in with my white family.'

As is often the case in adoption, split loyalties usually emerge on the part of some people and this was apparent in this group. One or two group members felt discomfort and said very little. As the facilitator I recognised the reluctance to join in with some of the more outspoken, often critical adopted people. Some people attempted to excuse their suffering both at home and in school, which they felt was compounded by their white parents' ignorance. Few denied they felt loved by their parents and siblings – some of whom were the natural children of the adopters. Most realised love was not enough and that a wide cultural and racial gap had been evident for some time. Many said they felt the "difference"; however, they were powerless to do anything about it. Although they recognised their feelings of isolation and loneliness, they were unable to express their feelings to their adoptive parents. When they did, they were either ignored or trivialised.

After a lengthy discussion one evening with the group, I posed some questions in relation to the type of support they thought may have helped them over the years. Members of the group, who had experienced breakdown, agreed that early intervention by a social worker who understood their needs could quite possibly have prevented the disruption of their adoption. They felt that intervention by a social worker would have been most effective if it was on a regular basis, i.e. two to four times each year after the adoption order was made. Some indicated that when social work intervention did take place, it was usually due to a problem which had developed into a crisis. Others felt that at that time, the young person was so consumed with anger, the intervention was ineffective. One or two spoke of being primed by their parents to express happiness and contentment in the family on the one occasion a social worker did visit, which was shortly after the adoption order was granted. They felt that an ongoing relationship with a familiar social worker would have allowed them the privacy to speak openly about their distress.

Others thought that if ongoing contact had been established, i.e. two or four times per year, family issues could have been discussed in their infancy, rather than exploding in late adolescence leading ultimately, in some circumstances, to total breakdown of the adoption. Most of the group felt that with early and continued contact with an identified social worker, some if not all of the issues around race and racism might have been dealt with in a way which would have sensitised their parents to their confusion and pain. They recognised that all adopted children have to deal with the stigma of being adopted at some point in their young lives, but there is the added stigma of being the only one in the entire family who is black. However, with social work intervention, preferably from a black social worker, there would have been an outlet for the isolated black child's anger. A young adopted person said that the intervention of a social worker, because of problems with his adopted sister, led him to make contact with the agency and begin the search for his birth family, a move which was positively encouraged by his adoptive parents.

Significant changes will have to be made in the adoption law if post-adoption support is to become an ongoing and important part of the adoption process, and not a one-off event. The availability of a social worker after adoption is not only thought necessary for black children in transracial adoptions, but for all children, black or white, in same race placements, because there are always questions that will arise which the child either cannot or will not ask their parents. Effective adoption is not only about how well the adopter/s are assessed; parenting skills and their sense of ownership must also be assessed.

The following poem was written for a young man who learned, at age 24, that he had an older sister. He was angry about his adoption which broke down during the teenage years. He was angry at being deprived of his culture. He was angry that he had never been told – even though he had sensed – that he had an older sister.

At last at last I'm not alone
My nightmares did not lie
The rage that burned within me deep
is slowly moving by

To know one's blood is somewhere else
just waiting to be found
Unless you're lost or in a search
you cannot understand

I had a letter from my sister
which was written in her hand
I wrote to her elated
At last I could expand

I had to meet her right away
to know that it was true
I'm not all alone, she is for real
She's in my life to stay

I couldn't wait to meet her
but the worker had a "plan"
I felt my anger rising
but they were in command

There are some things
you both must do
before you meet your "blood".
A film I think you both should see
It's called "Forbidden Love"

The days stretched on and on and on
Until at last we met
We hugged, we cried, we laughed we talked
At last I felt complete.

Mary Mac

22 **So where are you from?**

A black adopted person

So where are *you* from?

The question was inevitable yet I was always unprepared, disappointed. For most people this question would appear simply to be part of the course of a social conversation. I felt as if I were being interrogated, as though on trial for crimes of a constantly changing nature. I was being judged. I had to justify my existence, prove that despite having foreign features I was actually "white".

I grew up in a small rural market town. I was sent to "good" schools. I received much love and attention from my white adoptive parents. I used to cry a lot. I was told I was "sensitive".

Like most kids I craved the approval and acceptance of my peers, but they seemed so different to me. They seemed to know something secret. Although I had been told from an early age that I was adopted, that my African father and English mother could not look after me so I had been specially chosen, I did not really understand the full implications of being an "off the peg" baby. I remember going to a party organised by the adoption agency and being interviewed by a Radio 4 journalist on what it was like to be adopted. 'It means that I was specially picked out by mummy and daddy.' I was asked if I knew why I was a different colour to mummy and daddy. 'Because I have been in the sun too long,' I replied, much to the shock of my parents.

I wanted so much to look like the other kids in my class. In my eyes the main difference seemed to be my hair. The other boys I knew had brown hair, or blond hair, or red hair. Hair that moved as they moved. Hair that blew around in the wind into their eyes and mouths. Hair that they could hide behind. My hair was cut close to my scalp. My head looked like an egg. I felt exposed and alien. When I left home to go away to college I decided to see what would happen if I grew my hair, ironing out the crinkles with my travel iron. I no longer looked like an egg but I looked even more alien. I gave up playing with my hair and also gave up looking in mirrors. I removed every mirror in my flat. I stopped trying to look like anyone else. In fact I went out of my way to appear more alien. I wore odd clothes and listened to strange music. But despite this I was desperate for people to like me.

'So where are you from?'

'I'm from Buckingham. It is a small rural market town in the Home Counties.'

'Oh really! That sounds very nice . . . but where were you born?'

'In London, I think.'

'But I mean where are your parents from?'

'From Hampshire.'

'Oh really! I cannot help noticing that you have a bit of a tint.'

'Oh really! Where are you from?'

I finished my degree and moved to London. This was the first time I had really been near to Black People. I was near but I was not close. They seemed to know a similar secret to the people back home in my small rural market town. I could see vague physical similarities between myself and these Black People but I still felt very much like an alien. There were just more of us aliens.

'Hey, where are you from?'

'I'm adopted. I grew up in the country. My parents are white.'

I found myself a job. I found myself a partner. A white partner. I found myself with emotional and professional responsibilities. Three and a half years of juggling these responsibilities with my regular nervous breakdowns became a drag. I decided to find my *self*. Or more specifically, to find my natural parents.

As it turned out I did not have to do much searching. I contacted the adoption agency, who in turn were able to quickly contact my natural mother. She sent back a message saying she could not see what purpose would be served by my contacting her and as far as she was concerned the details of my father were something she wished to keep in her past. She was emphatic. The matter was closed.

Despite not getting the outcome I had wanted, I was comforted by the knowledge that someone had owned up to my existence. I had concrete proof that I was not from Mars. For the first time I actually felt I had something in common with the rest of the world. I found hope.

'Where are you from?'

'I'm black. My father is African and my mother is English. I'm also adopted. My adoptive parents are white.'

Last week I discovered that my partner's new car had been broken into.

'I'm so sorry about your car. I know how much it means to you.'

'I know. It is unfortunate, but I'm ninety-nine per cent sure the person who did it is your colour.'

I felt ashamed, angry, confused. My hope is gone.

'So Russell . . . where are you from? You look so exotic.'

'I'm not sure. But believe me, you don't want to go there.'

23 **Post-adoption issues in intercountry adoption**

Peter Selman and Sue Wells

Peter Selman is Head of Department of Social Policy, University of Newcastle. Sue Wells is an adoptive parent.

In many ways, the needs of the parents who adopt from abroad are no different from those of domestic adopters and in this respect the main concern is to ensure that they have equal access to the limited services available. This may well not be the case, as parents who have adopted overseas have usually had little contact with social services and no preparation for adoption, so that they may be less informed about available support.

However, intercountry adopters also have additional and particular needs, which arise from the special needs of children adopted from abroad as well as from the parents' different experiences in the process of overseas adoption. The aim of this chapter is to highlight these additional needs. In discussing these differences, we shall draw on the more extensive and better documented experience of overseas adoption in other European countries[1,2] and illustrate some of them from the experience of one of us as an adoptive parent in this country.[3]

The needs of children adopted from abroad
Studies in the USA and Scandinavia suggest that on arrival 'between one third and sixty per cent of older children display health, linguistic, behaviour and emotional problems',[4] although only a small minority fail to overcome their difficulties.

Health problems
Many children display acute health problems on arrival in their new country. Often they have conditions ranging from genetically determined disorders to parasitic infestation and intestinal problems, which may be

192

unfamiliar to medical practitioners in their new country.[5] A Dutch study of 116 Thai children[6] reported that 50 per cent of parents 'considered their child's health poor or even bad'; and 28 per cent of parents in a recent British study[7] said that the child's health was poor on arrival. Most seem to recover very quickly, but it can be a testing time for parents and the rare occasions when the child fails to recover are, of course, devastating for parents who have made a huge commitment of time, money and emotion in the process of adopting. The children often show retarded physical development, but this is usually made up within three years.[8] It is in this area that the gains of intercountry adoption (ICA) are perhaps most evident in the transformation of ailing malnourished children into fit and thriving young persons as a result of the dedicated personal care offered by the parents. It is, nevertheless, vital that progress is monitored and that parents are given all the medical support they need.

Language difficulties

Older children adopted from abroad may arrive in their new country with developed skills in a language they will never use again and have to learn a second language which is to become their primary language.[9] Even younger children have to start acquisition of their new language late, having experienced early communication in a very different context. All this is in addition to the problems of making new relationships with their adoptive family. Such children may adopt different strategies – from initial silence to 'crowing and babbling'.[10] In most cases difficulties of communication appear to be shortlived, but Gardell[11] reported a persistence of language difficulties in 43 per cent of overseas children adopted in Sweden.

Attachment disorders

Parents usually expect and cope well with problems of health and language in their child, but find it much more difficult to deal with emotional problems and in particular a lack of responsiveness. Hoksbergen[12] outlined some of the most common problems associated with adaptation to a new family and country: eating and sleeping disorders; lack of emotional response; lying and stealing; lack of concentration, etc. Difficulties are most apparent in older children:

Cederblad[13] studied 27 children who had been aged three or over when they arrived in Sweden. Most experienced either regression or crisis reaction during the initial months, and some displayed serious adjustment difficulties with four still showing serious emotional disturbance a year after their arrival in Sweden.

In some cases attachment disorders are so profound that professional help is essential. The existence of such problems in the Netherlands was underlined by the publication of a book by an adoptive parent entitled *Bottomless Existence*,[14] which gave a moving account of the difficulties faced when an adopted child fails to respond. This led to the use of the term *Bottomless Pit* syndrome – in which parents find themselves pouring love, energy, etc, into children apparently incapable of response. The Post Adoption Centre in London has reported similar problems with a minority of special needs adopted children.[15]

Loss of their birth country

Much of the concern about intercountry adoption has focused on the fact that it is often transracial, but in many ways the problems faced are as great for children adopted from Greece or Romania as from Colombia or Sri Lanka. The experience of British children separated from their parents and sent abroad to Australia and Canada is a reminder of this in our own history. The loss is a key factor in the problems of identity and lack of information discussed in the next two paragraphs.

Problems of identity

Many adopted persons face problems of identity,[16] but these are especially acute for those children who are adopted transracially or transculturally.[17,18] Dalen and Saetersdal[19] talked of adopted children feeling they had a 'Norwegian soul in a Vietnamese body' and a desire to distance themselves from more recent immigrants, notably the "boat-people". Andersson[20] has written movingly of the way in which those adopted from overseas cope with being an Indian-Swede or a Korean-Swede and feeling out of place in both countries. Parents need support in dealing with such issues, especially in adolescence, and the role of peer-support becomes crucial here, so that any successful post-adoption provision should build on the experience of parents' groups in linking couples who have adopted from the same country.

Lack of background information

Helping an adopted person with such problems is often made more difficult by the lack of information available. All persons adopted in Britain now have the right at the age of 18 to a copy of their original birth certificate and to request further information from court records. Much of the work of post-adoption services has been involved in helping adopted persons obtain such information and possibly use it in searching for their origins. For children adopted from abroad there is no such right and all too often even the most basic information is lacking. This is particularly true for children who are not adopted through an agency. One of the concerns of the Hague Convention was to ensure that in the future information is collected and available to adopted individuals as they grow up.[21,22] Even if there is information, the problems of making contact with birth families are likely to be greater than for children adopted domestically.

In Sweden there has been concern over the situation of children who have not been placed through agencies, as it is felt that often the parents feel hesitant about asking for background information on their child and there is also nowhere for the child to turn to when they grow up.[23] In the Netherlands, the 1988 *Act on Intercountry Adoption* requires agencies to keep files of information for at least thirty years after the adoption of the child, but makes no such requirement in the case of independent adoptions.[24]

Conclusion

Post-adoption needs can occur at all stages of adoption. Initially concern may be over physical health and regressive behaviour; later there may be problems of adaptation *outside* the family and especially at school; in adolescence there may be severe behavioural problems and issues of identity. Despite these extra difficulties most reviews of research into intercountry adoption[25,26,27,28,29] report mainly positive outcomes.

British adoptive parents' experience of adopting from abroad

Most of the special needs of children adopted from abroad are common to intercountry adoption in all receiving countries and many of the illustrations given are from evidence accumulated in other countries. In contrast, many of the difficulties facing British parents are peculiar to this country – or more generally to countries without a proper structure of agencies – so that the discussion below will make use of comparison with the situation of domestic adopters in Britain and of intercountry adopters in those countries with more advanced service structures.

Independent adoptions

Adoption from overseas in Britain has been almost entirely arranged by prospective parents without the support of any agency.[30] The practicalities of linking with the country of origin and bringing a child back to Britain tend to have depended on the energy and ingenuity of the prospective adopters.[31] Andersson[32] sees a major problem of independent adoptions being that there tends to be both a lack of preparation and a lack of background information. At worst independent adoptions may involve individuals motivated by profit; birth mothers who have not clearly given consent; and other dubious practices.[33,34]

Contact with social services departments

Prospective adopters of overseas children must undergo a home study by a social worker from an approved adoption agency. The contact with social workers is, however, often limited and unsatisfactory with many complaints from adopters of a negative attitude, a relationship distorted by payments, and a lack of understanding of ICA. Once the adoption is finalised there is rarely any ongoing contact. As a consequence, the contact with social services or their agents tends to be seen as transitory and seldom leads to any feeling that they can be turned to *after* adoption if problems occur. Psychiatrist Marianne Cederblad[35] notes the need for continuing support for those who adopt from abroad *after* the adoption, but also the very real resistance to seeking help of most adopters who were "independent, proud people". If this is the case in a country where ICA is accepted, "illegal" adoption rare, and there is little evidence of ambivalence, let alone hostility from professionals, how much more likely is it to occur in the UK!

Feelings of official disapproval

At worst the experience of social services and other bodies such as the Home Office is seen in negative terms. Adopters feel that their action in adopting from abroad is not approved. Parents in the International Bar Association study[36] spoke of hostile social workers and a feeling that they had to justify themselves all the time: 'We were made to feel guilty about adopting from abroad,' or 'We were made to feel we were smuggling A'. Such parents are unlikely to go to official bodies for help and may feel doubtful about the response they will get from independent organisations. In contrast, in the Netherlands and Sweden, intercountry adoption is accepted as legitimate and efforts are made to ensure that parents feel able to turn to the authorities for support.[37,38]

Lack of preparation

One of the most problematic features of the intercountry adoption process in Britain is that those who adopt from abroad tend to have very little preparation, in comparison with "domestic" adopters, despite the greater complexity of the adoptions they undertake. There are exceptions where home studies in Britain incorporate preparation courses[39,40] or where adopters have received guidance from parents' groups, but for most adopters from abroad there has been little formal exploration of the issues involved in ICA or of the problems that may arise after adoption.

Yet it is now widely agreed that 'if adoption is to work well, parents need to be carefully prepared for the arrival of their child.'[41] In his study of Thai children, Hoksbergen[42] wrote that 'well-prepared parents seem more able to cope with problems,' criticising the practice in the Netherlands of offering applicants only a few voluntary preparation sessions. This led to pressure on the Dutch government to introduce compulsory preparation courses.[43,44] The 1988 *Act on Intercountry Adoption* requires all prospective adoptive parents to attend the information and preparation programme run by a government agency [Bureau VIA] *before* they approach a Council of Child Welfare for a home study.[45]

Financial investment in adoption

Many parents adopting from abroad will have spent a large amount of their own money on solicitors' bills and travel. This is true of ICA in all countries and Sweden is the only country we know where the government has given financial support to those adopting from overseas.[46] In Britain many will also have had to pay for home studies, for which most local authorities now charge in contrast to Sweden.[47]

Backdoor entry and "illegal" adoption
The darkest side of intercountry adoption[48,49,50,51] is where there are doubts about the legality of the process and where there are questions about the consent of the birth parents, the motivation of intermediaries or the behaviour of the adopters. The large sums of money involved may lead unscrupulous lawyers to exploit childless couples, birth mothers to relinquish children in return for payments, and well-meaning but desperate couples to evade the law, as in the case of the British couple who tried to smuggle a child out of Romania in the boot of their car.

In extreme cases this may lead to children being brought in unofficially and never formally adopted. Where an "illegal" entry occurs, the authorities face the dreadful dilemma of whether to impose sanctions when this may further disrupt the life of an already traumatised child. This is vividly illustrated by the case of "Serena", a child illegally brought into Italy from the Phillipines, who was subsequently removed from her adoptive parents and placed in a children's home.[52]

Conclusion
The experience of many overseas adopters in Britain has been that they have had to do things on their own without the help of – and often in the face of hostility from – professionals. Access to post-adoption services is of vital importance, as many general services in Britain will have only limited experience of the problems of adopted children and often *no* experience of *foreign-born* adoptees.

What do families require from a post-adoption service?
In the previous section we noted some ways in which adopters from overseas face a different situation from domestic adopters in seeking help after adoption. In this section we look at what the adoptive parents themselves see as their major needs. For many much importance is

attached to being able to meet other couples who have adopted from abroad and to be able to talk to people who have gone through similar experiences. Often there is a particular interest in meeting couples who have adopted from the *same* country. There is a general reluctance to approach local authorities social services departments which are seen as likely to be at best lacking in experience of overseas adoption, and at worst unsympathetic or ideologically opposed. As a consequence, for many parents the main post-adoption support sought or received has been from the parents' organisations.

Hoksbergen[53] reported that 25 (22 per cent) of his sample of Dutch adoptive parents of Thai children had sought help – many more than for parents of Dutch born children – from medical practitioners, regional institutes for mental welfare, and other organisations. Evidence from other European studies indicates that eventually many adoptive families turn to professional help, but that typically this is deferred until problems are very acute. This is true despite a generally sympathetic attitude from professionals in those countries. It is likely, therefore, that many British parents who have adopted from abroad will need help at some stage, and an urgent need to ensure that they feel able to seek this and to find a sympathetic ear when they do so.

In the Netherlands, post-adoption support is encouraged through an organisation called *Werkverband Adoptie Nazorg* (Foundation Adoption Aftercare) which seeks to provide such support as part of children and family services generally, believing that adoptive parents do not want to be segregated from other families.[54] The foundation is funded mainly by the Ministry of Justice, but also receives support from the leading Dutch adoption agency, *Wereldkinderen* (Worldchildren).

A case study in the adoption of children from overseas

Sue Wells has twelve children altogether, six by birth, five from intercountry adoption, and one from a domestic adoption. Here she tells the story of some of the problems – medical, emotional and behavioural – they presented and of their experience of contact with their birth families.[55] She also talks of the problems in receiving appropriate support from services which were often hostile, suspicious or ignorant of intercountry adoption.

199

Case

We already had six birth children, the youngest a baby, when my husband and I first made positive steps to adopt after seeing distressing sights on television of children in the Third World. Our eldest birth child was eleven and our youngest three when we succeeded in adopting Peter and Victoria from Bangalore in South India.

When Peter and Victoria were two, we set out on the difficult path again, after seeing pictures of starving people in Ethiopia. It took several visits to the borders of Sudan and Ethiopia before we adopted Msai, and nearly three years before we received the letter telling us about twins, Gebre and Berhana, abandoned by their mother and desperately in need of a family. We immediately flew out to bring them home.

Peter and Victoria weighed just two pounds at birth. Their mother had no antenatal care and she left them at the hospital just two hours old. We knew about them soon after birth but spent a stressful time, worrying if they would survive, before adopting them at sixteen weeks. By then they weighed five pounds, were suffering from chest infections, severe eczema and scabies, but once in England, they made rapid progress, becoming healthy and reaching all their "milestones" early.

Integrating Peter and Victoria into the family was not a problem. They were accepted just as all our new babies had been on coming home from hospital after their birth. Victoria was upset to be taken from her familiar carer and both babies were unsettled by the time differences between India and England, but apart from these short-term problems, they adjusted well.

We adopted Msai in the Sudan when he was eight, but because of time-consuming "red tape" he was ten when he joined us in England. I saw him for the first time when he arrived at Heathrow, a little boy with thin wrists and a shy smile. His problems were different. His health was comparatively good but his life had been traumatic, first in war torn Eritrea, then in the horror of the famine camp amidst death, disease and despair. He had never been to school and spoke no English but threw himself wholeheartedly into becoming integrated. On the morning after his arrival, he put on his school uniform and went happily with the other children to the school which had been awaiting his arrival as excitedly as we had. Within a short time, despite language difficulties, he settled into family and school, made many friends and proved to be an able sportsman. Academically he has always struggled, and at eighteen, he has to cope with not doing as well as five older siblings who are all at university, but he is about to embark on a sports course at college which we hope will lead to future opportunities.

Gebre and Berhana, adopted at fifteen months, presented with the most severe problems, both medically and emotionally. Their first months of life were of repeated near starvation and abandonment. We were asked to adopt them when, at a year, they weighed less than the average new born baby. This we did in Khartoum, then travelled the eight hundred mile journey across the desert to collect them. On the bus back it seemed Gebre would not survive, he was so ill. Both babies had malaria and pneumonia as well as severe malnutrition, constant diarrhoea and sickness. We wondered if Berhana had suffered irreversible brain damage, but our main concern was to get back to England before they died. Later we would worry about other problems!

Once back in England, with good medical care, enough food, and a loving stable environment, Gebre and Berhana began to thrive. Initially over one and a half years behind, at four they had physically caught up, but the trauma of their first year had meant many problems. They had to learn to eat and, having done so, Gebre developed a passion for food so great that it dominated his whole existence, stopping him from making normal progress. He never played as all his energy was focused on obtaining food. He snatched food from the children's plates, raided the fridge, and ate anything from cat food to raw meat. Help was difficult to find: no-one seemed to have experienced such an extreme eating disorder in a baby, nor could the professionals quite believe it was as bad as I said. The paediatrician was sympathetic, recognising similar patterns of behaviour to those found in adults who had been starved. She referred us to a child psychologist for advice. One solution suggested was to continuously, over a period of two days, force feed him, but I felt this to be cruel and so could not do it. Eventually, I accepted that he needed to eat continuously and allowed him to, showing no interest even when, on numerous occasions, he ate everything and there was nothing left for the family! Many times I was filled with frustration and despair but eventually, as he realised food was always there and I no longer seemed to mind him taking it, he gradually became less obsessive.

The twins also had to learn to form attachments. At first Berhana was unable even to make eye contact but then became excessively clingy, insisting I carry her, crying "mummy" continuously and pulling my face towards her if I spoke to anyone. Although tiring, I found this easier to deal with. She needed reassurance that she would not be rejected as she had been in the past, and I was confident that she would improve with time and security. She did and by the time she started school she was happy to spend short periods away from me.

School can bring problems for children adopted from abroad. It is often the first time the racial difference from their parents is brought to their attention by those outside the family. I prepared the children for this and when Victoria was told by another child that I couldn't be her mother she was quick to correct her! She and Peter have always been happy at school, with many friends. They do encounter some racism now they are in senior school but we discuss it and, with family support, are strong enough to cope. Starting school for Gebre and Berhana, just when they were beginning to overcome their initial difficulties, seemed to create other problems. Unable to attend the same school as my other children they had to face racism from both white and Asian families, so severe that I was forced to move them to yet another school but the problems continued. Gebre was still suffering, to a lesser degree, from his eating disorder which meant he could not eat his dinner fast enough unless using fingers as well as a fork. This was mentioned by his teacher and she excused him saying 'I suppose it's inbuilt,' a racist remark I found totally unacceptable, especially from a teacher. Now they have joined the junior school their siblings attended and at last I feel they are accepted. They still have problems. Berhana is behind her peers in many ways and Gebre, although bright academically, lacks co-ordination and some social skills, but at last I feel able to share my worries with sympathetic teachers.

All the children have a good self-image, are proud of their racial identity and happy with their colour, black or white. While being honest about the reasons for adoption, we are positive, taking an interest in the literature, music and culture as well as the physical beauty of their countries, trying hard to balance the negative image portrayed by the Western media. The importance of this was brought home to me some years ago when we talked of visiting India and the children asked anxiously what we would eat.

Little is known about the birth families of either set of twins but we have maintained contact with those involved in their adoptions. If they wish to search we will be supportive, helping all we can. We have met all of Msai's family and keep in regular contact. When he was sixteen, Msai went back to Sudan to visit them.[55]

Adopting from abroad is difficult. You have to be determined and resilient. With all the children, contacts and arrangements were made by us. For Peter, Victoria and Msai we had prior entry clearance, but for Gebre and Berhana, because of their critical condition, we had to obtain this at the airport. This was frightening and stressful but, once aware of the reason, we found the immigration department helpful. They dealt with paper work quickly and effectively, enabling the twins to receive medical care without delay. I have not always found it easy to admit to having problems with the children or to ask for help. I am aware of social disapproval from some, even though without adoption at least two, and possibly four, of my children would have died.

The belief that under no circumstances should children be placed transracially makes it difficult and also affects the children. When he was very small Peter suffered great anxiety, believing that someone would come and take him away because he was black and I was white. Many people are under the impression that enormous amounts of money have been paid for the children and that illegal procedures have taken place. While in a few cases this may be true, for the majority of intercountry adopters it is not. We paid only court fees, medical care, and the foster mother when we adopted Peter and Victoria, and for the adoption of Msai, Gebre and Berhana absolutely nothing.

In common with others, I have not always found contact with social services comfortable. The feelings of disapproval from some social workers makes one wary of admitting to problems for fear of criticism. As all my children had to be adopted again in England, contact was unavoidable during their first year here. Unfortunately, because of their attitude, the help that I needed with Gebre and Berhana could not easily be asked for. In contrast, Charlie, the most recent addition to our family, was a domestic adoption. For the first time I have felt approval for taking a child into my family, even though I am now a single parent. The local authority responsible for the placement has been positive, helpful and fully supportive. I have felt able to discuss problems and ask for help when necessary and it seems wrong that when adopting from abroad the same, much needed support is not available. Attending a recently formed post-adoption group, I felt inhibited, fearful of disapproval, even though I had much to offer the group as the most experienced adopter there. This was because it was run by the local social services department.

It is important for post-adoption support to be available for those who have adopted from abroad and for those in need of help to be able to ask for assistance without fear of prejudice. I am a member of Stork and, as a group, we can compare experiences and support each other but, as the organisation is comparatively new, experience is limited mainly to small children, so that the help available is not always enough and more expert advice is sometimes needed. If attitudes can be changed and professionals educated about the particular problems faced, intercountry adopters could use the post-adoption services being set up by many local authorities. This would be of benefit to all adopters, with a wide range of experience and support being available within the groups. An alternative would be for organisations such as Childlink, which have a positive attitude and prepare parents for overseas adoption, to extend their programme to offer support after placement. However, this would still leave those who adopt from abroad in isolation, different and less acceptable to society and I believe that services shared by all adopters is what we and our children really need.

I now help at Childlink with preparation groups for those hoping to adopt from abroad. It was through Childlink I adopted Charlie and here I feel valued as an adopter, both intercountry and domestic. I am glad to pass on my experience to others, to give encouragement and advice and would like to see proper government channels for intercountry adoption. Providing the officialdom did not slow down the already lengthy process, it would be beneficial to all concerned, ensuring the best interest of the child and parents and much of the stigma attached to intercountry adoption would disappear. If it had been possible I would have wished to use such an agency.

Conclusion: future directions in the UK

Although there has been a growing interest in post-adoption provision in Britain,[56] there has been little attention to the needs of overseas adopters.[57] If, as some commentators suggest,[58,59] problems are most likely to arise some years after adoption, especially in adolescence, it may be some years before we see the full extent of need, as the larger numbers of children adopted in Britain since the late 1980s reach their teens. It is, therefore, vital to strengthen this aspect of post-adoption services *now* so that they are equipped to deal with such a demand in the years ahead.

In fact there is already evidence of a need for post adoption support for intercountry adopters in Britain, highlighted by reports of Romanian children being admitted to care following the breakdown of their adoptive placements.

For many of those adopting from abroad the main source of support has been contact with others in a similar situation through parents' groups. Stork, the Association of Families who have adopted from abroad, has concentrated increasingly on post-adoption support in recent years and holds regular seminars for its members. There are, however, signs that a growing number of parents are using the services of other organisations. The Post-Adoption Centre in London has found an increasing number of intercountry adopters attending its group meetings[60] and this has led to information on the service offered being included in a recent Stork Newsletter. Staff from the Centre have also addressed Stork seminars. After Adoption in Manchester similarly reports that a growing number of parents attending their group sessions have adopted from abroad. Childlink, which arranges home study reports for several London boroughs, has found that there is a clear interest from couples in keeping in touch after placement.[61]

However, even substantial improvements in post-adoption provision will achieve little unless we simultaneously address the need for improved preparation for those adopting from abroad. We are a long way from being able to offer the quality of preparation seen in the Dutch courses run by VIA,[62] but it seems to us important to continue to press for a proper system of "mediation"[63] and for home studies to incorporate a much greater degree of preparation as is evidenced in the work of groups like Childlink.[64] One step could be to develop a code of good practice for adoption workers, utilising the experience of such bodies and linked perhaps to a manual of guidance similar to the Swedish manual for welfare committees.[65]

Unless action is taken to ensure that not only are intercountry adopters not excluded from post-adoption developments, but that their special needs are recognised and provided for in the future through both post and pre-placement services, there is a real danger that we shall find a growing amount of distress in both parents and children in the years ahead.

References

1. Selman P, 'Intercountry Adoption: what can Britain learn from the experience of other European countries?' in Room G (ed), *Towards a European Welfare State*, SAUS, pp 151–186, 1991.

2. Selman P, 'Services for Intercountry Adoption in the UK: some lessons from Europe', *Adoption & Fostering*, 17:3, pp 14–19, BAAF, 1993.

3. Wells S, 'One Family's Experience of Contact' *Adoption UK*, no 68, Feb 1994.

4. Triseliotis J, 'Intercountry adoption: A brief review of the research evidence', *Adoption & Fostering*, 15:4, BAAF, 1991.

5. Clara R, and Eyckmans L, *International Colloquium on Health Problems of Foreign-Born Children*, University of Antwerp, 1988, Belgium.

6. Hoksbergen R, *Adopted Children at Home and School*, Lisse, Swets & Zeitliger, 1987.

7. IBA (International Bar Association), *The Intercountry Adoption Process from the UK Adoptive Parents' Perspective*, 1991.

8. Cederblad M, *Children Adopted from Abroad and Coming to Sweden after Age Three*, Solna, 1982, Sweden.

9. Hene B, *Language Development in Intercountry Adoptees*, University of Goteborg, 1988, Sweden.

10. de Geer B, 'Five adopted boys change languages' in Zaar C, *Intercountry Adoptions: What is the state of research and what new fields need to be investigated?* NIA, 1991, Sweden.

11. Gardell I, *A Swedish Study on Intercountry Adoption*, Allmanna Barnhuset, 1979, Sweden.

12. See 6 above.

13. See 8 above.

14. van Egmond G, *Bodemloos Bestaan: Problemen met Adoptiekinderen* [Bottomless Existence: Problems with adopted children] Baarn; AMBO, 1987, Netherlands.

15. Burnell A, Personal Communication, 1995.

16. Haimes E, and Timms N, *Adoption, Identity and Social Policy*, Gower, 1985.

17. Hoksbergen R, *Psychic Homelessness*, unpublished paper, University of Utrecht, 1994, Netherlands.

18. McRoy R, 'Significance of ethnic and racial identity in intercountry adoption within the United States', *Adoption & Fostering*, 15:4, BAAF, 1991.

19. Dalen M, and Saetersdal B, 'Transracial Adoption in Norway' *Adoption & Fostering*, 11:4, BAAF, 1987. Also, Saetersdal B, and Dalen M, 'Norway: Intercountry Adoptions in a Homogeneous Country,' in Altstein and Simon, 1991 (see 26 below).

20. Andersson G, 'To feel or not to feel Swedish – is that the question?' *Adoption & Fostering*, 15:4 pp 69–74, BAAF, 1991(a).

21. Duncan W, 'The Hague Convention on the protection of children and co-operation in respect of intercountry adoption,' *Adoption & Fostering*, 17:3, pp 9–13, BAAF, 1993.

22. van Loon J H A, *Report on Intercountry Adoption,* Hague Conference on Private International Law, April 1990.

23. Andersson G, Personal Communication, June 1993.

24. Bunjes L, *Foreign Adoption in the Netherlands: General Information and Preparation*, Maarssen, 1992, Netherlands.

25. Bagley C, *International and Transracial Adoptions: A mental health perspective*, Avebury, Aldershot, 1993.

26. Hoksbergen R, 'Intercountry adoption coming of age in the Netherlands: basic issues, trends and developments', in Altstein H, & Simon R J, *Intercountry Adoption: A multinational perspective*, New York, Praeger, 1991, USA.

27. Thoburn J, and Charles M, 'A review of research which is relevant to inter-country adoption' in *Review of Adoption Law*, Background Paper 3, Department of Health, 1992.

28. Tizard B, 'Intercountry Adoption; a review of the evidence,' *Journal of Child Psychology & Psychiatry,* 32:5, 1991.

29. See 4 above.

30. Selman P, and White J, 'Mediation and the role of "accredited bodies" in intercountry adoption', *Adoption & Fostering*, 18:2, pp 7–13, BAAF, 1994.

31. Humphrey M, and Humphrey H, *Intercountry Adoption: Practical experiences*, Routledge, 1993.

32. See 23 above.

33. See 22 above.

34. Pierce W, and Vitello R, 'Independent Adoptions and the "Baby Market"', in Hibbs E, *Adoption in International Perspective*, IUP, 1991, USA.

35. NIA (Swedish National Board for Intercountry Adoptions), *Legal Provisions Concerning Adoption*, 1991, Sweden.

36. See 7 above.

37. NIA, *Adoption in Sweden*, 1985, Sweden.

38. See 8 above.

39. See 2 above.

40. Childlink, *Intercountry Adoption Procedures for Referrals – Applications-Assessments*, Childlink, 1992.

41. See 25 above.

42. See 6 above.

43. See 2 above.

44. van Tuyll L, 'Intercountry adoption in the Netherlands: Compulsory preparation classes for new adoptive parents,' *Adoption & Fostering* 18:2, pp 14–19, BAAF, 1994.

45. See 24 above.

46. Andersson G, *Intercountry Adoptions in Sweden – the experience of 25 years and 32,000 placements*, Paper presented at International Conference on Adoption, Edinburgh, 1991.

47. Walby C, 'The Adoption Law Review – policy and resource implications' *Adoption & Fostering*, 19:1 pp 8–13, BAAF, 1995.

48. See 26 above.

49. See 17 above.

50. Landau E, *Black Market Adoptions*, F Watts, 1990, USA.

51. See 34 above.

52. See 1 above.

53. See 6 above.

54. White J, *Adoption in the Netherlands*, BAAF, 1993.

55. See 3 above.

56. Hughes B, *Post Placement Services for Children & Families: Defining the need*, Social Services Inspectorate, Department of Health, 1995.

57. Department of Health, *Adoption: the Future*, Cm 2288, HMSO, 1993.

58. Hoksbergen R, 'Development & Research in Intercountry Adoption, 1945 – 1990,' in Zaar C, *Intercountry Adoption: what is the state of research and what new fields need to be investigated?*, NIA, 1991, Sweden.

59. Verhulst F, 'Problem behaviour in international adoptees,' *Journal of the American Academy of Child and Adolescent Psychiatry*, Vol 29, 1990, USA.

60. See 15 above.

61. Hesslegrave C, Personal Communication, 1995.

62. See 44 above.

63. See 30 above.

64. See 40 above.

65. NIA, *Intercountry Adoption; manual for municipal welfare committees*, Swedish National Board for Intercountry Adoptions, 1989, Sweden.

24 Training in post-placement support

Sally Wassell

Sally Wassell is an independent social worker offering consultancy and training to local authorities and voluntary organisations.

Introduction

This exploration of some issues in post-placement support examines three different models of participation in a recent set of training courses organised for adopters and other permanent carers through the British Agencies for Adoption and Fostering (BAAF) in Scotland. The specific initiative involving numerous different courses separately funded is initially described in some detail, followed by a briefer description of two other patterns of training participation by way of comparison.

Throughout the text the term 'permanent carers' is used to encompass adoptive parents and permanent foster carers. The first model described involved a significant majority of adoptive parents, but many of the issues raised in long-term care of separated children have been seen to be shared by those permanent foster carers who took part in other recent training events.

The training project I will describe was part of a pilot project in post-placement support for permanent carers. The project was jointly funded by a grant from the Children in Need appeal and Strathclyde Regional Council Social Work Department. The project itself was organised through BAAF's Scottish Centre, based in Edinburgh, and was intended to meet the identified needs of permanent carers throughout the central belt of Scotland. Staff working in the BAAF Scottish Centre were becoming aware of the extensive demands both for training and for other forms of post-placement support following adoptive placements. We had noticed an increasing number of phone calls from families throughout Scotland who were experiencing particular difficulties in responding to the emerging needs of their older adoptive children, particularly those in the adolescent age group.

The survey

In order to research the needs of a wide range of adoptive parents, we mounted a postal survey by questionnaire of some 400 families. Many of these families lived in Strathclyde, Lothian and Central Regions of Scotland. We made a particular effort to make contact with families in Shetland in order to broaden our information base and to clarify whether the needs of the families in the central belt of Scotland were representative of the needs of families in rural areas. We chose Shetland because of our keen awareness of the high numbers of children from the mainland placed with families on the islands for adoption, and our involvement with these families suggesting parallel needs for post-placement services.

We sent an extensive questionnaire to the total group of families and received comprehensive responses within a fortnight from 120 families. From these responses, we gathered a great deal of useful information about the kinds of services which might usefully be offered through a pilot project, and further ideas for regional social work departments to address gaps in existing services. Many of the families which responded were caring for children who were at least in the early adolescent age group, but some were young adults still living with their adoptive families.

Overall there were a great deal of positive responses to the question-naire which asked about preparation of the families for adoption, preparation of and information about the children being placed, as well as a whole range of questions about the origins of post-placement support throughout the children's dependent years. We made a deliberate choice to ask families about their experiences of caring for the children throughout their dependent years rather than to focus on the issues of the tracing of birth family members, as this area of work is well covered by the local authorities and a specialist agency, Family Care, in Edinburgh.

Many of the families reported good experiences of parenting their adoptive children. It was indeed heartening to learn how many families had experienced great joy in rearing these children and overcoming significant hiccups in their development at particular stages, notably the stage when they were telling their children in more detail about their adoptive status, often as preschoolers; secondly, when they were integrating this information at late primary school age; and finally during the uncertainties of adolescence. It was no surprise to learn that even those families whose children were babies when placed with them had felt some need for particular kinds of specialist support at these key points. Noticeably, many families had managed without this support but were quick to add that this would have eased the parenting tasks for them. More than half the respondents indicated their pleasure in parenting, some further 25 per cent noted a number of difficulties which they felt were not insurmountable but had necessitated in engaging further help. A smaller but significant percentage, 10 per cent of the families, had experienced, and were continuing to experience, marked difficulties in continuing to care for their adoptive children, particularly in adolescence. The degree to which post-placement support services were available within their locality varied. It was interesting to note that when these could be located, specialist services had been particularly helpful. Positive support from school staff was very much appreciated, particularly sensitive guidance from teachers and educational psychologists. Social workers who knew the family well, and those who had worked for a long time with the children and therefore understood many of the issues coming from their early lives, were also significantly appreciated during the years after the adoption process. Clearly, some of the unmet needs emerging indicated that training was only part of the continuing of service which families wished to be made available to them throughout the children's childhoods.

In response to the survey, we structured a four-pronged service, largely for families in the central belt of Scotland. These included:

1. The funding of a number of self-help groups throughout the country.
2. The development of an information bank concerning the availability of professional services and local support which hopefully would serve the whole of Scotland.
3. The structuring of a multidisciplinary consultancy service to be offered to families from one work base in Glasgow and the other in Edinburgh over a period of six months;
4. A series of training events, some particularly geared to workers, but the majority focused on the needs of adoptive and permanent foster carers also in the central belt of Scotland.

Both the multidisciplinary consultancy service and the training courses offered to workers and families were researched by Janice McGhee, a research worker at Edinburgh University, Department of Social Policy and Administration. The results of this survey are separately published by the Scottish Office and in articles for *Adoption & Fostering*,[1] and a study published in 1995, titled *Developing Post-placement Support*, examines these and assesses them.[2]

The trainers
Several different trainers took part in the training sessions for permanent carers. The session on loss in adoption was run by a counsellor experienced in transactional analysis, who also had also vast experience of running parent effectiveness programmes and who is herself a permanent carer. Feedback from this session certainly underlined the awareness of the participants of the resonance of the trainer's own experience.

Other sessions were run by two workers experienced in work with permanent families and with children at different ages and stages, living separately from their own families. The theme of these sessions was "Understanding and Managing Difficult Behaviours". The sessions focusing on caring for children who had been sexually abused were run by a worker currently in practice in this area of work in a partnership with a worker experienced in fostering and adoption. The session on caring for adopted adolescents was run jointly by a specialist in work with young people and an experienced fostering and adoption worker.

Content
The choice of the particular topics for this series was largely chosen from the survey of families' identified needs for training. All the trainers had considerable experience of working with permanent carers and understood the need for a practical approach combined with readily accessible theoretical material. The request from participants for an emphasis on skills and techniques, particularly in behaviour management, was very marked.

Methods
The methods used in the range of courses for carers varied from large group presentations by course leaders, through small groups for

discussion and exploration of a particular set of difficulties with an individual child, to role play and video. Those participants who experienced the role play exercises were particularly appreciative of this way of translating practical difficulties into the training setting. Handouts were provided and these were frequently very much appreciated by course participants, and where they were not available, this was lamented.

The training courses
The training courses offered to parents and/or carers were as follows:

Loss and adoption
This was a day-long course exploring a theoretical framework underpinning an understanding of loss and grieving in children. It also explored the parallels in the carers' experience and the ways in which these can be intertwined in permanent substitute care – either adoption or permanent fostering. Participants enjoyed the opportunity to apply the theoretical framework to the live situations in their families. The feedback demonstrated that they gained an increased understanding of their child, as well as aspects of their own lives.

Parenting the child who has been sexually abused
This was a two-day course for carers which focused on a combination of understanding the nature of the child's experience of living with sexual abuse, and providing the essential features of a nurturing environment within a substitute family setting. This course was run twice owing to the high demand. Comments on the course included an appreciation of information offered which helped families to feel more confident in dealing with this issue in placements.

Caring for adolescents who have been sexually abused
Owing to administrative problems, there was only a small group of participants for this course, although there was a great deal of interest in the topic and participants commented that they wished they had had more time to explore the issue further. The conjunction of problematic issues of the search for identity and the re-emergence of anxieties about past

abuse at this stage of development was a major feature of this course.

Adoptive fathers – parenting and support

This was only a half-day opportunity for adoptive fathers to get together and was extremely lively. There was a recognition of the real value for adoptive fathers to get together to discuss issues common to their perspective on parenting their adoptive children. This illustrated the degree to which the role of the male carer is complex and an often neglected issue.

Adoption issues in adolescence

This course was not primarily skills-based but explored some of the developmental issues with particular relevance in adolescence. In general, the feedback reflected an appreciation of the opportunity to gain more knowledge, but, as was the case in the other issue-based rather than skills-training course, more practical ideas would have been valued.

Understanding and managing difficult behaviour

This was a two-day course and, because of the level of interest, was held twice. The course focused on harnessing the understanding of the significance of sources of difficult behaviour in individual children and young people with the techniques for managing this behaviour. As the focus for the course was at least partly to encourage skills development and techniques for behaviour management, this aspect was particularly appreciated by carers.

Looking at the courses overall, particular features emerged as especially valuable to participants.

1. In general terms, it was noted that the courses which focused primarily on the development of practical skills and techniques for behaviour management were especially valued by participants. Many of the carers volunteered during these courses that they had had little available advice as to how to approach understanding and then managing the behaviour of their adopted children, particularly those in the throes of adolescence.

2. The ideas which were valued were not only those of the course leaders, but also those offered by colleague carers.

3. What seemed to be of particular value for the carers was the offer of series of frameworks for making sense of the child's experience which then gave them a tool which they could use, not only in dealing with the current problem, but also to apply to any future difficulties. The significance of this seemed to be its effect on confidence-building.

4. Although the courses were based very much in the central belt of Scotland, ie. Glasgow, Edinburgh or Stirlingshire, a number of carers came from very far afield, for example, the Islands and Dumfries and Galloway. Informal feedback from these participants, since the courses were held, has underlined the significance of an opportunity to join with other carers when one lives in a rather more isolated rural area. This was, incidentally, a valid and significant comment in relation to the multidisciplinary consultancy service, where families who would otherwise not have easy access to a multidisciplinary group of professionals found it a great comfort and support to discover their own experience was similar to that of many other adoptive families.

5. We made a particular decision not to involve carers and workers in the same training courses. Several participants informally commented that they would have liked their own support workers, or the workers for the children, to have been present at the courses so that they could have moved forward together with a shared understanding of some difficult issues.

Training courses for professional workers
The courses run for professional workers were as follows:

Effective parenting
A two-day workshop for professional workers involved in supporting families. This course was run twice.

Working with young people who have been sexually abused
A two-day course for professional workers supporting abused children in adoptive families.

Caring for the sexually abused adolescent
A one-day workshop for professional workers which was run twice.

Adoption issues in adolescents
A one day workshop

It is of interest that the workers who attended the courses were just as enthusiastic as the carers about gathering new skills in behaviour management, informed by a deeper understanding of particular issues. Informally, workers commented on the existence of numerous courses which offer an explanation of the significance of the problem but stop short of identifying particular techniques for work either with the families or directly with the children themselves. This would seem to point to the potential value of developing such practical skills-based courses in the future. A framework for understanding, allied to the exploration of particular skills in behaviour management, would seem to offer a potentially useful model which could be transferred from the immediate situation or problem to future difficulties. Some carers declared their intention to introduce frameworks offered, for example, in understanding and managing difficult behaviour, for use with their support groups in their local areas.

Other models of training participation
Two other models of course participation or membership presented themselves for comparison with the model used in the post-placement support pilot project.

Carers attending courses with their own support workers
At least one Scottish regional local authority uses this model in organising some of the training for both temporary and permanent carers.

Typically, courses involved carers engaged in similar caring tasks, with temporary or permanent care of children broadly within the same age group, so that issues/themes common to particular stages of development may be considered in greater depth, for example, the challenges of caring for adolescents on a permanent basis or the temporary care of younger children who have experienced significant abuse.

A recent example of such a model involved six adoptive families with their link workers attending two-day training sessions. The local authority involved favours this model and participants come to the course with real problems which they wish to use the session to address. A pattern which has been used is to spend the first day exploring key sets of ideas or approaches to understanding the issue in focus, followed by the exploration of a framework for rehearsing ideas, skills and techniques for practical application on the second day.

Feedback from course members over a number of different training events showed the particular value of carers and workers training together. This was seen most clearly in the following instances:

- When the course content focused on the use of the particular theoretical framework combined with practical ideas;
- When there was clear opportunity to focus in depth on examining the issues for a particular child and planning in detail for their care.

A common theme for participants was the unsatisfactory nature of a one-day course in dealing with any problems for carers in significant depth. Participants commented favourably on courses which are of longer duration and which provide a series of sessions at regular intervals or at least a follow-up session from a two-day course. This would appear to allow the learning to be continued, checked out and sustained more satisfactorily.

Individual children

In a recent piece of work in one of the Scottish regions, I was asked to undertake a series of training sessions focused on supporting the carers of a group of children (siblings and cousins) with very particular difficulties. Many of these difficulties arose from abusive experiences and were complicated by significant delays in aspects of the children's development. There exists a high level of commitment by the agency to supporting the families by providing for regular meetings. This is of particular value because of the importance of maintaining contacts between the children. The potential value of bringing the carers together to think through and plan various aspects the care of the children, rather than merely responding to crises, provided enough opportunity for incorporating training input on several key issues which could be integrated into the direct work with, and the care of, the children.

These sessions included the five couples caring for individual children, their own support social workers and the workers with responsibility for the children. The sessions ran for three whole days, at monthly intervals, the emphasis being on exploring key themes in work with separated children and providing frameworks to help carers make sense of the individual experience with the child in their care. In between sessions, carers were given 'homework' which invited them to make observations of their children's development and behaviour, and to contribute a focus on behavioural difficulties of key importance at a particular time. The sessions incorporated opportunities for the carers to glean what was relevant from particular theoretical presentations in the session and to apply these ideas to their own circumstances.

Of real benefit to the carers was the opportunity to think through problems, not just for their individual child but to reflect upon the resonances with other children placed with colleague carers, and with whom their own children have contact. Over the sessions, this built a heightened atmosphere of co-operation, not only with other carers, but also with the children's workers. The sessions provided a focused opportunity to collect together much of the relevant detail of the children's background and incorporate these into the planning for daily care in a realistic way.

The workers reported their increased awareness of the daily difficulties of caring for each of the children, and the key elements of importance in planning contact between them was not only highlighted but explored in detail. All the carers at the end of the sessions indicated their satisfaction in expressing and exploring the challenges of caring for their own particular child. This increased the atmosphere of collaboration between them and their colleague carers. The trainer facilitated the negotiation of the direct contact between the children from a clear focus on the purposes of the contact and the way this could inform how the link happened and what boundaries were essential to promote its effectiveness.

The trainer introduced to the whole group sets of ideas which it was hoped would be applicable to the particular circumstances of the carers and the children living with them. The focus of the work was on building the practical application of these ideas in a way that invited the carers and workers to model the application in the sessions, and returning to test out any difficulties or snags at the ensuing meeting. Having once tested the relevance of the framework for approaching behaviours (several taken from Emily McFadden's[3] work in foster care training), the families declared themselves more confident in approaching future behaviour problems.

What they took from the sessions was an increased awareness that underlying issues of abuse and neglect had different effects on each child, varying with temperament, age and stage, nature of abusive experiences, and that these underlying issues were vital in informing a particular choice of behaviour management technique.

It must be said that this was a group of carers living with children with particularly challenging behaviours as a direct consequence of severe abuse, who felt rather inhibited speaking openly in their local carer groups because of local knowledge of the children's families. They repeatedly fed back that it was freeing for them to be able to discuss particular issues with other carers facing similar challenges. Since the training sessions, the links between the carers have continued.

Although the training sessions for the post-placement support pilot project generally included larger groups of carers (up to 18 or 20 maximum for two trainers), the smaller size of the group in the latterly described exercise was of particular benefit because it enabled more of a detailed focus on the challenges of dealing with very troubled children.

Conclusions

From the three different models of training employed, it would appear in the first case from researched data, and the last two examples from written post-course feedback, that there are some features of training for permanent carers which may be of particular value.

1. That the training should preferably involve a trainer who is experienced in the realities of the long-term stresses of caring for severely troubled children on a permanent basis.
2. That the opportunity for those carers who feel themselves to be geographically isolated of meeting with other carers is particularly welcome.
3. For carers who are dealing with unusually complex problems which involve severe behavioural and developmental difficulties, it may well be of some value for them to join with other permanent carers outwith

their own region for specialist training sessions.

4. That carers most appreciate training which is of a practical nature and which addresses directly the problems they are struggling with day to day.

5. That ideas and techniques which they can rehearse in the training session and later take home with them for further use or take into their own local support groups, may be of particular benefit. This approach not only builds their confidence, but also helps them not to feel over-whelmed when facing severely distressing behaviours of a persistent nature.

References

1. McGhee J, 'Consumers' Views of a Post-Placement Support Project', *Adoption & Fostering*, 19:1, BAAF, 1995.

2. Watson L, with McGhee J, *Developing Post-Placement Support: A project in Scotland*, BAAF, 1995.

3. McFadden E, *Fostering the Child who has been Sexually Abused*, Michigan Department of Social Services, E. Michigan University, 1986, USA.

Conclusions

Rena Phillips and Emma McWilliam

Rena Phillips is Lecturer in Social Work, Department of Applied Social Science, Stirling University. Emma McWilliam is Professional Officer, Adoption and Fostering, Central Region Social Work Services.

We undertook to edit this book in the belief that the development of post-adoption services must be planned through understanding the needs of those directly involved. It was therefore important for us to seek contributions from adoptive parents as well as to promote the views of service users and those practitioners who, through their experience of working alongside adoptive families, are able to speak on their behalf. For many of the adoptive parents this was the first time they had ever written about their experiences. We want to acknowledge the fact that this was often at some personal cost in reawakening unresolved and painful feelings. However, they were determined to do so in order that future adoptive families could benefit from what they had learned. Through sharing their different post-adoption experiences, common themes have emerged which become more powerful as they are reinforced through each chapter and have the overall effect of clear messages about the kind of post-placement and post-adoption services adoptive families need. From this vein of information, we would like to highlight some issues which seem particularly important for the future planning of services.

Continuity of experience and of service for adoptive families, which finds expression in the concept of "through placement care",[1] emerges as a vital element of effective practice. There is a danger that terms such as "pre-placement", "post-placement" and "post adoption" are treated as separate stages, rather than responding flexibly and imaginatively to the needs of adoptive families at any particular time. Just as the granting of an adoption order can no longer be seen as an end in itself, so effective post-adoption services begin at the point of placement. At the very least, adoptive parents need to know where to turn for help, be aware of the options open to them if they start to identify problems later on, and be given an assurance that any future request for help will not be viewed as a sign of failure. Some placements will need a comprehensive support package to be in place from the outset. This may take various forms: financial help such as adoption allowances, a properly organised respite scheme, therapy and counselling as a right both for adopted children and adoptive parents, and ongoing training to accumulate the necessary skills and coping mechanisms. A recurrent theme identified by families and practitioners is the importance of a full assessment, often of a multidisciplinary nature, of all children registered for adoption. This would have prevented some of the traumatic experiences related to us by adoptive parents who subsequently discovered that their child had a severe attachment disorder or long-term problems resulting from early deprivation and abuse. We have the knowledge and experience to make predictions about the extent of a child's future difficulties. The belief that a few years spent in a loving secure family will repair the emotional damage of a child's early years is no longer tenable. Adoptive parents should be starting out with more realistic expectations about the task they are taking on and the likely outcomes.

The lessons we are learning about the post-placement experience of adoptive families point to obvious similarities with the needs of long-term foster families. Increasingly tougher demands are being placed on permanent substitute families as they care for the most damaged children and young people in society – the challenge of coping with children with high emotional and developmental needs, the fight for their educational rights and opportunities, helping the development of racial and cultural identities, and the complexities involved in maintaining contact with birth families. Whilst there are concerns about the level of support provided to long-term foster carers, the contractual nature of their relationship with placing agencies means that they gain access to resources in a more routine way. If post-placement support continues to concentrate on long-term foster placements we should not be surprised if adoptive parents raise questions about whether they would be better off offering themselves as long-term foster carers rather than adopters.

We are conscious that this book does not adequately give voice to the views of adopted children and young persons in relation to post-placement support. This is a reflection of the fact that whilst there has been progress in the development of post-placement services for birth parents and adoptive parents, there is a gap in the provision of services to adopted children and young persons in their own right. Most of what we know about their emotional and developmental needs when placed on a permanent basis comes from, and is mediated by, the experiences of people such as substitute parents, birth parents and practitioners. Whilst sharing many common needs, the wishes and feelings of adopted children and young persons will be affected by their disability, gender, race and culture. In the move towards more openness and contact in adoption, we need particularly to hear their views on how they can achieve both a sense of permanence and a clear sense of personal identity. They have a right to expect that their opinions will be taken into account in deciding the way that scarce resources are distributed. For example, would they want a key worker outside their adoptive family or a support group they could attend? Should these groups be run by practitioners or adopted people with appropriate counselling skills? It is time children and young people had a real say in the future of post-placement services.

The organisational changes taking place within local authorities, and with it the move to new smaller units, raise inevitable questions about the delivery of post-placement and post-adoption services. Will these authorities have the necessary specialist resources to provide services themselves or will they need to band together in some form of consortia arrangements? Some local authorities currently purchase a range of post-adoption services from specialist voluntary agencies such as the Post-Adoption Centre in London.[2] A recent development between the latter and one social services department is a new model of post-placement provision summed up as the 50/50 principle of collaborative and complementary service provision. The local authority maintains a broad responsibility to provide post-placement support but does so in partnership with the Post-Adoption Centre as the independent and specialist services provider.

Whatever models are followed in planning future post-placement services, the twin imperatives of continuity of service and a co-ordinated approach, rather than piecemeal provisions, should be the guiding principles. This can only be achieved if we continue to listen to the voices and expertise of service users, act upon what they ask for, and work alongside them. In a future clouded by funding and policy constraints, we are reminded by an adoptive parent that adoptive families are still our best resource.

References

1. Hughes B, *Post-Placement Services for Children and Families: Defining the need*, Social Services Inspectorate, Department of Health, 1995.

2. Burnell A, and Briggs A, 'The next generation of post-placement and post-adoption services: a complementary contract approach,' *Adoption & Fostering*, 19:3, BAAF, 1995.